SHANGHAI FLAIR

上海本真

The Vision of a French Chef in China

法国大厨的中国美食之旅

Nicolas A. Vienne 著

—Michelin Chef & Culinary Designer 米其林厨师 & 美食设计师

SendPoints

Part II
Downtown Shanghai

Must-try Shanghainese Dishes

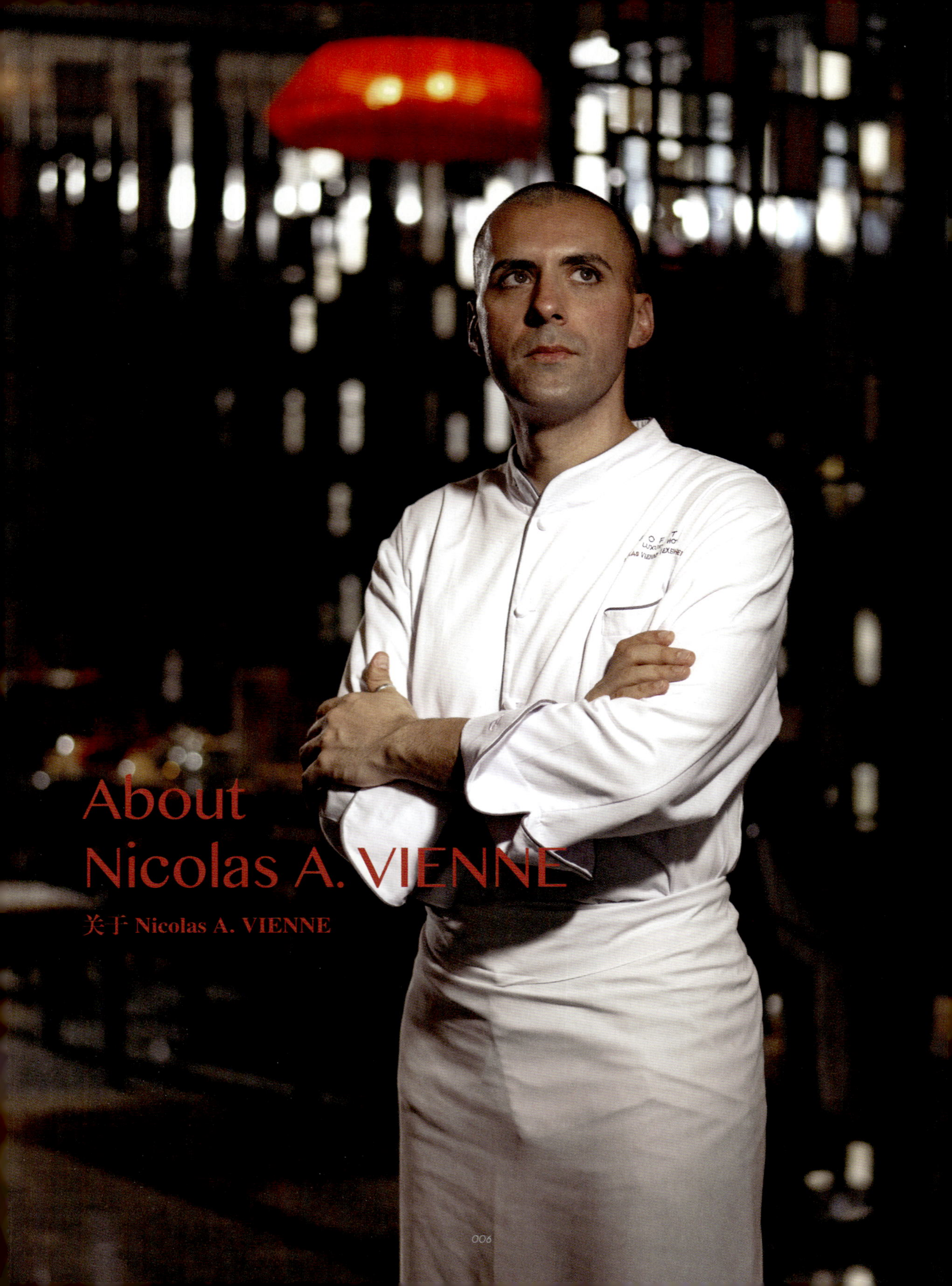

About Nicolas A. VIENNE

关于 Nicolas A. VIENNE

France, 1994-2000

I started my apprenticeship in Paris, France with two culinary schools where I received training from the most famous establishments in Paris, including George V, Bristol, Plaza Athenee, Alain Ducasse, and Le Crillon. My passion for cooking started in 1990 when my family taught me some recipes and took me to local places in France where delicious food waited to be discovered.

North America, 2001-2002

After six years of study in France I moved to the USA to finish my Bachelor's degree in Rhode Island. During that time I got my first job as a chef in Boston where I stayed two years to open a French organic bistro in the financial center.

From Middle East to Florida, 2003-2006

Beirut, the capital of Lebanon, was my next trip in 2003 as a chef for a French luxury brasserie. I stayed there several months and then came back to France. With a strong desire to open my own business, I left for Miami in 2005 to open a large catering shop followed by a bakery. It was an amazing but quite difficult experience.

From Miami to the Pacific, 2006-2009

In 2006 I moved to the hotel resort in New Caledonia, an impressive place for me to discover new products and local food, where I took charge of a hotel for the first time. My story with Sofitel group started in Bora Bora in 2007 when I was in charge of three hotels, a challenging but rewarding experience again. I had a great time in paradise with the fish in the lagoon, the freshness of the products, and the friendliness of the local chefs.

Asia, 2009 to present

I was lucky to have worked in Shanghai from 2009 to 2011, during which Shanghai hosted the World Expo. I was able to discover a new culture, exotic street food, new products, and also engage in a food and beverage operation that was much bigger than the previews ones.

Being awarded as the most innovative chef honor by the Accor group in 2011 was really an unusual experience for a young chef in the group.

Then in 2011, I was relocated to Bangkok to open a new Sofitel hotel. It was an interesting experience to be the main actor responsible for creating a brand new standard and also participating in an amazing adventure. After six months of preparation, the grand opening for this new hotel in downtown Bangkok was highly successful. Then I moved back to China to work with the Sofitel in Guangzhou, a new city to provide new challenges, successes, press releases, interviews and citations in the culinary guides.

法国，1994–2000

我在法国巴黎的两家烹饪学校开始了我的学徒生涯。期间，在巴黎最著名的乔治五世四季酒店、布里斯托尔酒店、雅典娜广场酒店、阿兰·杜卡斯餐厅、克里伦酒店接受培训。我对烹饪的热爱始于 1990 年，那时，我家人常教我做菜，带我去法国各地探寻美食。

北美，2001–2002

在法国学习六年后，我到美国的罗德岛来完成我的学士学位。在这期间，我在波士顿得到了第一份厨师工作。为了在金融中心开一家提供有机食品的法国餐厅，我在那儿待了两年。

从中东到佛罗里达，2003–2006

2003 年我来到了黎巴嫩首都贝鲁特，在一家法国豪华餐厅里担任主厨一职。几个月后，我回了法国。在一股想自己开店的欲望推动之下，2005 年，我前往迈阿密，先开了一家大型餐饮店，然后又开了一家面包店。这段经历颇为艰难，但同时也使我振奋。

从迈阿密到太平洋岛屿地区，2006–2009

2006 年我来到了新喀里多尼亚的度假酒店区，第一次全权负责一家酒店的管理。这地方令我印象深刻。我在那里发现了新的食材，并研究当地的美食。我和索菲特酒店集团的缘分始于 2007 年的波拉波拉岛，当时我在那里管理着。这又是一个颇具挑战但回报丰厚的经历，我过得非常开心，潟湖里畅游的鱼、新鲜的食材、当地厨师的热情，让人仿佛置身天堂。

亚洲，2009 年至今

我有幸在上海世博会期间在上海工作，见证了上海转型的重要时期。我有机会可以探索一种新的文化，享受异国街头小吃，接触新产品，从事远比之前更大规模的酒店餐饮管理。2011 年，我被雅高集团授予最具创新力厨师的称号。对这个集团内的年轻厨师而言，这是非比寻常的。

2011 年，集团将我派到曼谷筹备一家新的酒店，为该酒店创制全新的餐厅服务标准。这项新挑战，对我来说也是一次有趣的体验。筹备了六个月，酒店在曼谷市中心成功开业。然后，我回到中国，在广州索菲特大酒店工作。新的城市带来新的挑战，挑战过后是接踵而来的成功。在一个接着一个的新闻发布会、媒体访问和各种城市美食指南出版中，我也在努力去了解这个城市，体验这里的文化。

"Each recipe in this book has a story of its own. I hope you will enjoy both the stories and the recipes. Food without a story merely fills the stomach without nourishing the soul."

Introduction

by Nicolas A. VIENNE

开篇

I have travelled to countries across the continents. The things I have seen and experienced make me who I am today and allow me to see things, people and especially culture as a cross-cultural communicator first, then as a French chef on a search for perfection.

Working in Shanghai from 2009 to 2011 while the World Expo was being held there, I took on a number of little adventures around Shanghai, determined to discover a culture that was completely new to me. Local Chinese traditions that were once unfathomable to me gradually began to make sense. Street food and new types of produce excite a laowai chef like me.

Neither locals nor strangers see Shanghai as a city of profound culture because the cultural elements are eclipsed by the hectic pace of its economic development. I believe the cultural foundation of a city defines that city. As a chef, I see a connection between food, culture and people. In this book, I intend to show people that Shanghai is not only built on skyscrapers, technology, fashion, fancy cars and loud KTVs. For me, the heritage of Shanghai centers around a perfect mix of western culture with Chinese traditions--given how its history was written.

I want to bring attention to the true Chinese culture in different cities. The first stop is Shanghai, because Shanghai opened the first chapter of my stories in Asia. Also, it is the city that made me fall in love with China. I desire to share some of my recipes while telling the stories. Both the recipes and the stories say something about how I have become who I am today, my French cultural origins and my background as a chef.

Each recipe in this book has a story of its own. I hope you will enjoy both the stories and the recipes. Food without a story merely fills the stomach without nourishing the soul.

我游历过世界各大洲的许多国家，一路上我所看到的和经历的都丰富了我的人生。看人看事，我首先是通过一个跨文化沟通者的视野里去理解，然后才是从一个法国主厨的眼界去感受。

2009 到 2011 年间我在上海工作，期间上海举办了世博会。那三年里，我利用闲余时间游历于上海市区和市郊，去感受和了解属于这个城市的独特文化。曾经陌生又令人费解的当地传统和中国文化渐渐开始显露其中的深厚韵味。从老上海的街边小吃到各种新奇食材，无一不让像我这样的一个“老外”主厨兴奋不已。

在上海，无论是本地人还是外地人大多都没有将它看成是一个拥有深厚文化传统的城市，因为经济发展的狂热步伐使得这个城市的文化元素日渐挣扎在铜臭味中，艰难地呼吸着。我认为一个城市的文化根基是其最基本的层面，它定义了这座城市。作为一名主厨，我看到食物与文化、与人之间不可割舍的联系。在《上海本真》中，我想告诉人们，上海拥有的不仅仅是摩天大楼、科技、时尚、豪车或喧闹的KTV。对我来说，或多或少是由于上海的特殊历史，这个城市的魅力在于她体现了西方文化和中国传统文化的完美融合。

我想通过一系列关于中国城市的书来向世人展现真正的中国文化。这个系列的第一站是上海，因为上海开启了我在亚洲的故事。同时也因为上海是一座让我爱上中国的城市。在讲诉故事的同时，我分享了一些由我创作的食谱。你们会发现阅读这些故事、食谱，就像在阅读我的人生一般，因为它们都是我人生的一部分，携带着我的法国文化根源、我的厨师背景、我一路走过的点点滴滴。这一切，我都愿意和你们分享。

这本书里的每一个食谱都有一个故事，我希望你们会喜欢这种有故事的食谱。我想，没有故事的食物就只是食物，填饱了胃却不能滋养灵魂。

NICOLAS LE BEC INTRO

NICOLAS LE BEC 介绍

42 years old chef with 25 years of culinary experience, named as the Best French Chef in 2002, creator of famous restaurant concepts with multi Michelin Stars. Passionate about travels, cultures and worldwide food, left France in 2012 with his Chinese wife to open Villa Le Bec in Shanghai, a charming French place with a Chinese spirit.

现年 42 岁的 Nicolas Le Bec 有着 25 年的烹饪经验，并于 2012 年被列为“最优秀的法国大厨”， 还参与了多家知名米其林餐馆的创意构思。热爱旅行、文化和世界各地美食的他在 2012 年与他的中国妻子一起离开法国定居上海，经营以地道法国美食和中国本土味道而闻名的 Villa Le Bec 餐厅。

Culinary Photographer: Vincent Ho

美食摄影师：Vincent Ho

Preface

序言

There have always been chefs in search of tranquility while the extraordinary ones prefer adventures and explorations.

All times are marked by Food Corsairs, the adventurers of the taste, and flavors explorers who are always willing to understand, to learn, to exchange know-how and sharing of their emotions in an ethnic mix.

While many are proud of nowadays technological innovations and epoch-breaking inventions, few are taking the plunge to explore the tastes on five continents to see for real that nothing is invented but everything can be modified and mixed with the time.

The "laowai", as we are called in China, Nicolas Vienne remains a pioneer in search of wonderful Chinese food products and special Chinese culinary techniques. He possesses the unusual quality of a chef who is willing to go out of his kitchen and to search the best quality products to present to his guests and share his insights gained in his adventures.

China is a beautiful country, rich in history and culinary culture, a huge territory that offers the greatest variety of food products to those who are willing to look closer and dig deeper.

So Nicolas Vienne in Guangzhou and I Nicolas Le Bec in Shanghai, are working to offer our passion of great French cooking with a Chinese touch in this book. The journeys to exploring the food and culture of Chinese cities start from the gourmet tours, stories and specially designed recipes presented here in Shanghai Flair.

The next stop in the series would be about Guangzhou, an excitingly vibrant coastal Chinese city. Michelin Chef Jacques Pourcel and writer/food lover Donia Belhacene will join Nicolas Vienne in the tours around Guangzhou to discover the best food products, best locations, stories and recipes.

Enjoy.

从来都有喜欢在厨房里寻找安宁、享受安逸生活的厨师，真正卓越的大厨却总是乐于在未知领域中探索，勇于冒险。

为美食倾尽毕生热情的人给时代留下了他们追逐美食的印记。他们为味蕾的跳跃而跳跃，为舌尖上的感动而感动；他们有着阔达的心态去接纳不同文化中的酸甜苦辣，他们不断学习，在学习中分享，融会贯通，以食物的美名打造最高境界的文化甚至民族大熔炉。

科技创新和日新月异的发明见证了人类创造力带来的奇迹。从味觉上来说，倘若有人愿意深入探秘全球各地美食，他们会发现其实在这个世界，没有任何东西是被创造出来的。这些伟大的创新发明成果几乎都发酵于知识的沉淀、经验的积累，同时又被一个时代的特有风味点缀。

中国人喜欢称我们为“老外”。老外 Nicolas Vienne 是个不折不扣的美食文化先锋，他致力于发掘优质中国食物原料和中国烹饪技艺。与其他大厨不同，他积极投身厨房外的世界，搜寻最优质的食材烹调美妙的菜肴，并与大家分享旅程中的动人故事。

辽阔美丽的疆土、悠久的历史文明和独特的美食文化赋予了中国品类繁多的食材。但是，最好的食材永远只眷顾那些用心追逐的有缘人。

正是带着这样一颗诚挚的心，现居广州的 Nicolas Vienne 和定居上海的我决定通过一个系列的中国城市美食文化图书来分享我们怎样把纯正的中国味道融入精致的法式烹饪。这个系列始于本书《上海本真》，展现这位法国大厨的上海美食文化之旅，与读者分享他在上海市里市郊的点滴，以及他亲自设计的菜肴配方。下一站，米其林厨师 Jacques Pourcel 和作家 / 美食爱好者 Donia Belhacene 将与 Nicolas Vienne 一起去探索美丽而充满活力的海港城市—广州的美食与文化。

Traditions & Respect

China has, throughout history, been a country that pays great attention to courtesy, with the Chinese culinary culture deeply rooted in China's history. Visiting a Chinese home or restaurant you will find that table manners are essential, and the right amount of courtesy displayed will invariably help to make your visit more enjoyable.

I think the Chinese custom of taking care of the elderly, children, and guests at the table is very admirable. Chinese households are heavily influenced by the traditional Eastern Confucian view of filial obligation, which places the responsibility of caring for and respecting the elderly on the children. It is considered a moral duty. The practice of presenting the best or finest food first to the senior members of the family has been observed for generations. In ancient China, even when life was difficult, destitute Chinese workers would strive to support their aged parents who, most of time, would take it for granted.

Although the hosts in China are often friendly and hospitable, you should do your part as well in showing them respect. Before starting your dinner, the host may offer a few words of greeting. You should not start eating until the host says, "Please enjoy yourself" or something similar; otherwise such an action would suggest disrespect and incur displeasure.

The main dishes are usually arranged at the center of the table with complementary dishes placed evenly around them. The decorative elements, if any, on the main dishes would usually be placed facing the guests or the elders, which is also a way of showing respect to them.

Highlights on Chinese Culture

中国文化点津

传统与尊重

历史上的中国一直是一个非常注重礼仪的国家，而中国烹饪文化则深深地根植于其传统礼仪。因此在一个中国家庭做客或在中餐厅吃饭，餐桌礼仪很重要，恰当的礼节能让大家在愉快的氛围下进餐。

我很欣赏中国人尊老爱幼的传统。在餐桌上，他们会给老人、孩子和客人特别的关照。中国家庭深受东方传统儒家的孝道观念影响，他们认为成年子女有义务照顾和尊重他们年长的父母，并把最好的食物首先让给家里的长者。在古代中国，生活再贫困再艰难，人们也会尽最大努力供养他们年迈的父母，父母也认为这样的供养是理所当然的。

在中国，虽然主人家通常既亲切又好客，但同时你也应该表现出对他们的尊重。开饭前，主人家一般会说一些祝福语，在他们说完前不要动筷，否则会招致不满。

主菜通常会被放在桌子中央，其他菜肴围绕着主菜放在周边。当主菜带有装饰性配菜时，这种配菜一般会面向客人和或家里的长者，以示对他们的尊敬。

On Chopsticks

The history and culture of chopsticks stretch back many centuries and find their origins in China. The tradition of using chopsticks as tableware was introduced to many other countries in the world such as Vietnam, North Korea and South Korea.

The invention of chopsticks reflects the wisdom of Chinese ancient people. A pair of chopsticks, regardless of its plain appearance, can nip, pick, rip, and stir food. Nowadays, chopsticks are considered to be lucky gifts for marriage and other important ceremonies.

As history shows Western civilizations have used forks and knives for only about six centuries, thanks to the Queen Catherine of Medicis, who introduced these tools in France. Afterward, these utensils became a symbol for the monarchy in Europe.

For me, I now more frequently use chopsticks in restaurants, even in Europe, because it is much easier to use those simple wooden sticks.

When I cook I also use chopsticks, but they have their limitations in the kitchen. Sometimes it is more efficient to use traditional cutlery to prepare the dishes. In Chinese kitchens they still use them but the process is sometimes quite long and intricate. Usually there are more than a few people in a Chinese kitchen; so working at a slow pace is not viewed as detrimental. This to me is something that needs to be changed.

I think, with time, things will change in China.

Important Moments

Like people anywhere else on earth, the Chinese see birthday as an important occasion. When one is young, usually he will have noodles on his birthday, because the long noodles indicate longevity in China. When he gets older, his birthday will be celebrated in a more proper manner. In addition, peaches in many forms will be added symbolizing longevity and immortality, as well as delightful couplets and candles.

On the wedding day, it is also customary to serve dates, peanuts, longan and chestnuts together as a wish that the couple will soon have a baby. All these food has something that related to the Chinese word "zi", which usually means son.

To most Chinese people, returning home

筷子

筷子起源于中国，它的文化历史可以追溯到许多个世纪以前。

使用筷子作为餐具的传统被介绍到世界上其他许多国家，如越南、朝鲜和韩国。

筷子的发明反映了中国古人的智慧。一双筷子，不管外表多朴素，可以夹起、挑捡、撕扯、搅拌食物。如今，筷子被看做结婚和其他重要仪式上的幸运礼物。

历史表明，西方文明使用刀叉的历史只有六个世纪。梅第奇凯瑟琳女王将刀叉介绍到法国，随后，这些餐具成为欧洲王室的象征。

现在在餐厅吃饭，甚至在欧洲时，我都更频繁地使用筷子了。使用这些简单的木棍挺容易的。

我做菜时也用筷子，但在厨房，筷子有它的局限性。有的时候，使用传统刀具准备菜肴效率更高。在中国厨房，厨师大多数时候还是用筷子，用时却很长，各种动作的效率都不高。在我所了解到的中国厨房通常有好几个人，似乎手脚慢一点、效率低一点也无关紧要。

我想，随着时间推移，中国这些状况也会改变。

重要时刻

庆祝生日是人一生中的重要时刻。除了当天要吃生日蛋糕之外，人们一般在生日前还会吃一碗面，因为面条在中国文化里象征着长寿。

中年之后，人们会更加精心准备生日—添置各种形式的桃子以代表长生不老，也会贴对联，摆蜡烛。

婚礼当天，按照习俗会在新房摆放红枣，花生，龙眼和栗子，在中国的风俗里这寓意这早生贵子。

对于大多数中国人来说，返乡和离乡是两件大事，与之对应地也会有相关的饮食风俗。一般来说，返乡的时候吃面条，离乡的时候吃饺子。这在中国东北部特别盛行。

端午节期间，尽管很多人无法到河

after a long absence and the departure from home are both significant. There are dining customs associated with this. People returning home are greeted with noodles and those leaving home bidding a farewell are offered dumplings. This is especially popular in northeast China.

During the Dragon Boat Festival, though many people cannot reach the river zone to watch the famous dragon boat race, most of them would eat zongzi, a pyramid-shaped dumpling made of glutinous rice wrapped in bamboo or reed leaves to celebrate this traditional Chinese festival. The festival is to venerate the patriotic poet Qu Yuan who committed suicide by jumping into a river broken-hearted by the downfall of his country in B.C. 278. His people, fearing his body would be eaten by fish, threw Zongzi into the river to feed the fish so that they wouldn't bite Qu Yuan's body. Now Zongzi is made in various shapes and with different fillings.

On the eighth day of the last month in the Chinese lunar calendar, people will enjoy a nourishing porridge called 'La Ba Zhou'. In ancient times, monks would kindly share all sorts of grains with people and made them flavorful porridge on this particular day. People still keep this convention.

In China, when a baby is born, the happy father will send red boiled eggs to announce the good news. Eggs with a black pointed end and dots in an even number such as six or eight indicate a boy's birth; those without a black point and in an odd number like a five or seven means that the baby is a girl.

The festive Chinese new year's eve is usually celebrated by family gathering and a good meal in which fish is usually used to suggest the accumulation of prosperity and wealth at the end of a year.

区观看划龙舟比赛，但是绝大部分人都会吃粽子— 一种用糯米制成并包在竹子叶或芦苇叶里的金字塔形“饺子”。过端午节是为了纪念爱国诗人屈原。古时候，人们担心屈原的躯体会被鱼群啃食干净，于是大家把粽子扔进河里喂鱼以确保屈原的身体不再受侵食。现在粽子的外观与类别各式各样。

农历腊月的第八天，人们会享用一种营养丰盛的粥，叫“腊八粥”。在古代，和尚会好心将各类谷物分发给众人，并用这些食材在腊月初八这一天做成美味可口的腊八粥。现在人们还沿袭这种习俗。

在中国中部，一个婴儿降生之后，孩子的父亲会通过寄送红煮蛋来宣布消息。如果蛋有黑色尖头并且点呈偶数分布，那就说明是个男孩；如果没有黑色尖头并且点呈奇数分布，那就意味着是个女孩。

除了以上这些，鱼总是被人们用来象征繁荣和财富的积累。因此，在中国的除夕之夜团圆饭里总会有一道用鱼做的佳肴。

Shanghai Must-know

上海须知

Quick History of Shanghai

上海简史

5th Century

At the beginning Shanghai was a small fishing village.

起初上海只是一个小渔村。

12th Century

Shanghai became a trading place.

上海发展成为一个贸易场所。

15th Century

The Ming government started the construction of the old towns in Shanghai.

明朝政府开始进行上海老城区的建设改造。

17th Century

First contact with the Jesuit

上海初次与耶稣会接触。

At the end of the Ming dynasty Shanghai was well-known as a cotton and textile market place.

明朝末期上海以棉花及纺织品贸易闻名。

18th Century

During the Qing Dynasty Shanghai became a strong rival of Suzhou in trading business.

清朝期间上海在贸易领域成为苏州的强劲对手。

19th Century

Shanghai became a strong global competitor in the textiles, silk and fertilizer markets.

上海在纺织品、丝绸、肥料市场上成为强大的国际竞争者。

The Britannic started to be interested in establishing their colonies in Shanghai. The beginning of the fast development.

大不列颠帝国在上海兴起建殖民地。经济飞速发展。

UK opium trading and first opium war

英国的鸦片贸易以及第一次鸦片战争。

France, USA, Germany also started the Business

法国，美国，德国也开始在上海拓展地盘。

Beginning of the concessions age

租借时代开始。

Several conflicts happened

冲突与战争爆发。

20th and 21st Century

Shanghai became the " The Small Paris of the East and the Small Small New york of the West"

上海成为"东方巴黎 & 西方纽约"。

Shanghai become one of the biggest city of the world in 1936 with 3, 000,000 peoples.

1936 年上海成为当时世界上最大的城市之一，拥有人口 300 万。

The Shanghai war started in 1937.

1937 年上海战役爆发。

Many conflict with the Japanese pushing out the foreigners during the second world war marked the end of the concessions on 1946 (the last concession in Shanghai was the French concession.)

二战期间与日本人的多次斗争驱逐了外国人。1946 年租借时代结束（最后一块为法租界）。

From 27th May 1949 Shanghai has been under the control of the Chinese Communist Government.

从 1949 年 5 月 27 日起上海处于中国共产党的统治之下。

1950-60 Shanghai become a huge industrial area.

1950–60 年上海成为一个庞大的工业区。

1991 The Deng Xiaoping reform brought Shanghai back to the market and made it a global economic zone.

1991 年的邓小平深化改革上海重返贸易市场，使其发展成为全球经济重地。

2010 Shanghai hosted the world expo.

2010 年上海举办世博会。

Shanghai Cuisines

上海菜

Shanghai Cuisine, also known as Hu Cai, includes two styles - Benbang Cuisine and Haipai Cuisine.

上海菜，也称沪菜，包括两大风格—本帮菜和海派菜。

Benbang Cuisine, 'the local cuisine', is the traditional family style cuisine that first appeared in Shanghai over 100 years ago. Using fresh fish, chicken, pork and various vegetables as the main ingredients, it has a great flavor and a bright color with the use of oil and soybean sauce. Like the food of Suzhou and Wuxi cuisines, Benbang food tastes fresh, tender and sweet.

Haipai Cuisine, 'the all-embracing cuisine' is derived from the cosmopolitan culture formed in Shanghai at the end of the Qing Dynasty (1644-1911). It has absorbed the advantages of food from other regions of China and even western food, with adaptations suited the local tastes. Fresh fish, shrimps and crabs are the main ingredients of Haipai Cuisine. The appearance, flavors and cooking techniques of the Haipai dishes have many variations.

本帮菜，顾名思义就是指上海的乡土菜肴，是一种已经在上海存在超过百年的传统家庭菜式风格。采用鲜鱼，鸡肉以及各类蔬菜作为主料，在油和酱油的烹饪下总是香味满溢，色泽明亮。与苏州菜无锡菜相似，本帮菜滋味浓郁鲜美，清淡素雅，甘腴甜润。

海海派菜，字面理解即是“包罗万象的菜肴”，于清代末期（1644−1911）在上海形成的都市文化中诞生。它汲取了中国其他地区许多菜肴的优点，甚至也收纳了西方美食的优点，并将其经过改造后适应了本地的口味。海派菜的主料为鲜鱼，虾，蟹。菜肴的外观，风味以及烹饪技巧多样。

"Melting pot" cuisines can be found in all the Megalopolis all over the world. Paris is also a city where many different food cultures from the different regions influence the original style of the Paris cuisine. It is the in New York and Los Angeles as well.

Benbang Cuisine and Haipai Cuisine have much in common: First, they make great use of fresh meat, chicken, vegetables and especially various marine ingredients such as fish, shrimps and crabs; second, they have a great number of signature dishes made from various seasonal ingredients; Third, a wide range of cooking techniques have been adopted, including steaming, braising, stewing, stir-frying, quick-frying, deep-frying, boiling, marinating, smoking and roasting. Four, strongly-flavored hot food hardly ever forms part of Shanghai Cuisine.

In recent years, Shanghai Cuisine has been greatly influenced by Cantonese cuisine. Consequently the foods are now less oily and more delicate with the use of higher quality and more expensive ingredients. People here have become more conscious about healthy diet. There is an upsurge in the trend towards the use of fresh ingredients and fruit and vegetables of higher quality.

在全球各大都市都有不少不同菜系相互融合的现象：在巴黎，世界各地的饮食文化影响了本地美食的原本风味。在纽约和洛杉矶也有类似的饮食融合。

本帮菜和海派菜有许多共同点：第一，它们都擅长使用鲜肉，鸡肉，蔬菜，特别是各类海产品如鱼，虾和蟹来制作菜肴；第二，它们有许多来自当季食材的招牌菜；第三，两种菜式中都运用了各式各样的烹饪方法，包括蒸，炖，烩，炒，爆，炸，煮，腌，熏和烤；第四，上海菜中少有重口味的美食，大多数菜肴吃起来都味道鲜美，清晰，清淡，甘甜或带点微辣。

近年来，上海菜深受广东菜影响，所以现在上海菜变得少油，在采用更多高品质且昂贵的食材后也变得更加清淡。这里的人们已经更加重视饮食健康，这将意味着新鲜食材的使用将引领新的趋势，专注于高品质水果与蔬菜。

The melting pot cuisines

菜式大熔炉

Part I
Outskirts of Shanghai

第一部分 上海市郊

1

故事一

Organic Shanghai

有机上海

In Shanghai, farmer is not the most glamorous title.

When I was working in Shanghai, I noticed that my team did not really appreciate the farmers from the countrysides of Shanghai and other provinces.

Every day in my kitchen my staff said to the farmers, "Hey peasant... I need this, and I need that." Their attitude first seemed very strange to me. After several months, I discovered that most "proud Shanghainese" had no clue about the value of their countryside since they were too busy focusing on technology and fashion in the hustle and bustle of downtown Shanghai. I think it is unfortunate that most of them seem to have lost hold of their own cultural legacy. They overlook the real sense of life and forget how the life of their parents and their grandparents was like.

在上海，农民并不是什么光鲜的头衔。

在上海工作的那段时间，我的厨师队伍似乎对于来自上海郊区和其他省份的农民既不欣赏，也不感激。在我的厨房里，每一天都能听见工作人员对农民们嚷嚷道："嘿，乡下人…给我这个，给我那个。"这种蔑视的语气让我很不解。几个月后，我渐渐发现，骄傲的上海人大多一心追逐高科技和时尚潮流，而对于上海周边的情况则一无所知。让我觉得痛心的是，他们似乎已经丢失了属于他们的文化遗产，忽略了生命的真正意义，忘记了他们祖辈父辈的生活状态。他们对生命的感知、生活的体悟逐渐在繁忙的步伐中变得麻木。

Going Organic

有机时代的开启

In 2009, I brought an organic trend to my team and to Shanghai. If it were a few years ago, most of the chefs I know would have laughed at my attempt to start the first organic hotel in Shanghai. Yet, after several months of work in the farms and with the suppliers to locate safe food products, I would say the attempt was successful. One step at a time, I educated my team about the important things about farms and organic food, the meaning of culture and history.

I worked with organic produce suppliers to help develop their business and improve the quality of their products; I even brought seeds from France to grow new fruits and vegetables. One of the steps I took was growing a small garden in the hotel I was working for. The bigger challenge back then was the chicken project. Some suppliers in France have the perfect chicken but as always, high quality has a price. My target was to bring to the Shanghainese inexpensive seasonal products. For a decade in china, safe poultry supply has been an issue. High consumer demands for chicken have made product quality the last priority for some increasingly pervasive American fast food giants. At the time, it seemed almost impossible to find on the market high quality free range chicken of 81 days.

2009 年，我给我的厨师队伍和上海这座城市带去了一股有机食物浪潮。要是在几年前，大部分我所熟知的厨师都认为我要在上海开办第一家有机酒店的想法很可笑。然而在各个农场奔波了几个月，跟数家供应商进行沟通之后，我终于找到了放心的食材来发展构建有机酒店这个想法。我在潜移默化中给我的同事讲解农场和有机食物的重要性，和他们分享历史文化的珍贵内涵。

我与有机食材供应商合作，帮助他们发展业务，提高产品质量。我还亲自带来了种子，种植一些新品种的果蔬并在我工作的酒店里弄了个小菜园。那时，鸡肉的供应来源颇伤脑筋。一些法国的供应商有优质鸡肉供应，但高品质背后是昂贵的价格。

我希望为上海人寻找应季而价格合理的食物原材料。在中国，近十年来，优质家禽的供应一直是个问题。由于市场需求量巨大，一些遍地兴起的美国快餐业巨头优先考虑的绝对不是鸡肉的质量。要在市场上找到高品质的放养 81 天的鸡几乎是不可能的事。

在中式烹饪上，人们偏好嫩鸡，因其肉质鲜嫩。然而，我发现大部分我去过的上海农场无法供应优质的鸡肉。没有合理安排的喂养和优质饲料，鸡肉的质量难以保证。几个月后，我碰到了一个用有机种子和蔬菜养鸭的供应商，便想到了和他合作养鸡。

要找到优质品种的鸡并不容易，最终我们选择了广受中国消费者推崇的黑脚鸡。我的客人对用这种鸡熬制的高汤赞不绝口。六个月后，我们开始以每月

In traditional Chinese cuisine, younger chicken is usually more popular for the tenderer texture of the meat. However, most of the chicken forms I have visited in Shanghai do not supply high quality chicken. Without good food consistency control and proper care, high quality chicken is not possible. Months later, in meeting with a supplier who was feeding his ducks with the leftovers of organic seeds and vegetables, I got the idea to do the same with chicken feeding.

It wasn't easy trying to select the right chicken breed. In the end we chose the black feet chicken which is highly appreciated by the Chinese food lovers. The guests I have served in the hotel loved the double boiled chicken soup for example.

Six months later, we set off higher scale production with 600 free range chickens per months. They are fed with grain and vegetable on a safe soil. The system works and the chicken has become our key recommendation at the all-day dining restaurant at the hotel.

600 只鸡的规模进行放养，提供谷物、蔬菜和安全的土壤。结果令人满意的，在我工作的酒店，这些鸡肉成为了全天候餐厅的主打产品。

Recipe 1
食谱 1

organic chicken
有机鸡肉

Ingredients
配料

2 kg --------- Organic chicken (drumsticks, wing and breast)
有机鸡（鸡腿、鸡翅和鸡胸）

3 tbsp/ 汤匙 -------------------- Organic Olive oil 有机橄榄油

Salt/Pepper 盐 / 胡椒

Soy sauce (a dash) 少量酱油

1 tbsp/ 汤匙 --------------------- Dry Lemon Powder 干柠檬粉

250 g ---------------------- Portobello Mushrooms 双孢蘑菇

Vegetable side
蔬菜配菜

30 g ----------------------------- Organic asparagus 有机芦笋

30 g -------------------------------- Organic carrots 有机胡萝卜

30 g -------------------------------- Organic Zucchini 有机节瓜

30 g ---------------------------------- Organic Celery 有机西芹

30 g ---------- Organic small Chinese cabbage 有机娃娃菜

30 g ------------------------- Organic snow peas 有机荷兰豆

0.5 g -------------------------------- Confit Baby garlic 腌渍蒜

You can pick any 6 different vegetables.
可以任意 6 款不同的蔬菜

Mashed potatoes
土豆泥

600 g ------------------------------ Organic potatoes 有机土豆

150 g -- Butter 黄油

Seasoning 调味品

XO sauce "relish"
XO 酱

5,000 g -- Blend oil 调和油

500 g ------------------------------ Minced dry scallop 碎瑶柱

150 g ------------------------------- Shredded ham 火腿(幼丝)

50 g ------------------------------------ Dry chili pepper 辣椒干

100 g -------------------------------- Minced salted fish 咸鱼茸

100 g -- Dry shrimp 虾子

250 g ------------------------ Dry small shrimp 虾米（湿碎）

50 g ----------------------------- Minced Da Di fish 大地鱼末

5 g --- Salt 盐

150 g -- Chili oil 辣椒油

10 g --- Chicken flavor 鸡精

100 g -- White sesame 白芝麻

Lemon powder
干柠檬粉

The zest of 2 lemons 两个柠檬的皮碎屑

Directions
作法

1. Lemon powder:

Make a very thin brunoise (diced cubes of 1mm by 1 mm), dry it in the oven at 120°C for 1 hour, and leave it dry on top of the oven. Then blend it in the robot coupe.

干柠檬粉：制成非常薄的 1 毫米 ×1 毫米的小丁，放入 120 摄氏度的烤箱中烤 1 小时，放置在炉上风干。然后放入搅拌机中混合。

2. Chicken:

a. Pan sear the breast until it is lightly browned; pour on top some oil with a spoon to keep it moist.

b. Pre heat the oven to 180°C; baked the drumsticks for 15 minutes.

c. Deep fry the wings at 180°C till they are crispy.

d. Season with salt and dashes of light soy sauce. Add the lemon powder at the end.

e. Prepare the vegitable sticks, blanch them in boiled salted water (7 g salt per liter). Cool the vegetables down in ice water to keep their original color before stir frying them in the same chicken pan; Add soy sauce and the chopped coriander.

鸡肉：a. 煎鸡胸直至着色，时常在顶上用勺子倒些油使其保持湿润。

b. 预热炉子至 180 摄氏度，把鸡腿焗 15 分钟。

c. 用 180 摄氏度的油炸鸡翅至变脆。

d. 用盐和少许淡味酱油调味。最后放入柠檬粉。

e. 准备好蔬菜条，用盐水灼（每升 7 克的盐），然后用冰水降温以保留颜色。用煎鸡胸的锅炒，最后加入酱油和香菜碎。

3. XO sauce:

a. Boil the blend oil to 180°C-200°C.

b. Add minced dry scallop to deep fry them till dry.

c. Add minced salted fish to deep fry them till dry.

d. Add dry small shrimp to deep fry them till dry.

e. Add the shredded ham, minced Da Di fish, dry shrimp; deep fry them for 2 minutes.

f. Add some dry chili peppers.

g. Add chicken flavor and salt as seasoning.

h. Add the chili oil and white sesame.

XO 酱：a. 烧调和油至 180℃ –200℃。

b. 加入瑶柱碎浸炸至干身。

c. 加入咸鱼茸炸至干身。

d. 加入虾米碎炸至干身。

e. 加入火腿丝，大地鱼末，虾子，炸 2 分钟。

f. 加入辣椒干。

g. 加入鸡粉，精盐调味。

h. 最后加入辣椒油和白芝麻即可。

4. Finish:

Arrange the chicken and the vegetables; sprinkle the lemon powder and a spoon of the XO sauce on top.

收尾：把鸡肉和蔬菜摆放好，撒上柠檬粉和一勺 XO 酱。

Your notes

Great recipes are not created, but perfected.
好的食谱来自一次又一次的修改完善。

Note down the changes you make on this recipe to create your very own version of it.
记录下你对这个食谱做的修改，探寻属于你自己的味道。

Chef's tips 厨师贴士

How to choose your chicken?

The price of the chicken depends on what the farmers feed them with. And the chicken feed results in different color of the chicken meat and its taste and texture as well.

For me, I use free range chicken with an average weight of 2 kg. After cooking, if the chicken flesh comes out of the bones too easily, it means the meat is not of high quality. I would say you should always use farm-raised and free-range poultry.

如何选择鸡肉？

鸡肉的价格取决于喂鸡用的饲料，吃不同的饲料长大的鸡会有不同的鸡肉颜色和不同的肉质。我经常使用自由放养的，体重平均 2 公斤的鸡。如果烹煮后鸡肉容易脱离鸡骨通常说明鸡的质量不高。我建议大家尽量购买农家放养的家禽。

2

故事二

The Malu Vineyard

马陆葡萄园

The uncharted vineyard territories

Malu is known for its vast lands of vineyards, an experimental and growing base of the Malu Grape Institute which is the first professional research organization in suburban Shanghai approved by the Shanghai Commission of Science and Technology. It has so far introduced 38 species of grapes since its founding. Main attractions of the vineyard include the grape corridor, petite fruit orchard, wine castle, lovers paradise, miniature garden, fruit-picking garden and water-borne vineyard. Visitors can taste grapes of top quality, while visiting the farmers' vineyards nearby. The fun of picking grapes and enjoying home dishes at the farmers' homes has made the Malu vineyard quite a getaway destination of the locals.

葡萄园新世界

位于上海嘉定区的马陆因其众多的葡萄园而闻名，其葡萄园是马陆葡萄研究所的实验种植基地。该研究所是由上海科技委员会批准，设立于上海郊区的第一家专业葡萄研究机构。自成立以来，它已成功培育出了38种葡萄。葡萄园中的主要景点有：葡萄长廊，葡萄小果园、葡萄酒城堡，情侣葡萄园，葡萄盆景园，葡萄采摘园和水上葡萄园。在那里，游客不仅可以品尝到优质葡萄，还可参观农民葡萄园，既有动手采摘葡萄的乐趣，又能体验农家菜。马陆葡萄园是当地民众周末放松的好地方。

Countryside Vineyards

乡间葡萄园

It was surprising to find in the north of Shanghai more than 40 hectares of vineyards not far from the formula one race track. I have seen in the vineyards 12 types of grapes in different shapes for different use (for fruit consumption or for wine-making). I even discovered a unique one from Italy that looked like green Chili but it is so sweet.

All the grapes are carefully wrapped with paper bags for protection. No pesticide is used. The shapes of the trees offer a lovely view for a weekend getaway. Among all the vineyards, there is a small French style one that extraordinarily impressive, given its location in the Shanghai countryside.

Visiting the vineyards, I was wondering why these good quality grapes were not sold on the market. I didn't understand why the Chinese have to import those low-quality ones from Chili or the US. Later I was told that was because the Chinese didn't trust the quality of Chinese grapes.

In Shanghai the only grapes I could find grown in China was the huge ones that no one wants to eat. During the Chinese grapes seasons you can only buy those big red thick skin grapes that are not sweet and probably are covered with pesticides. But I was not surprised because we have the same issue in Europe. In France, the supermarkets import grapes from outside the country while we overproduce the grape just to throwaway for quota issue, because somehow in Europe produce quotas are set to balance import and export.

The oldest vineyard in Malu has a history of over 30 years. I met a farmer whose family has been working in the vineyards since his grandfather's times. The development in the vineyards is exciting and he believes the generations after him will sustain the growth of this green land. Local Chinese government allows them to keep the lands to develop better vineyards, which I believe is a positive sign of government support in China's agricultural development.

Before leaving the vineyards, I was curious what they do with the grape leaves. They use them as vegetable in some egg dishes. This has inspired me to create my version of vineyard egg rolls.

令人感到意外的是，我发现一级方程式赛道附近居然有一处占地逾 40 公顷的葡萄园。在这里，我看到了 12 个品种的葡萄，它们形状各异、用途不同（食用 / 酿酒）。这里还有我在意大利见到过的一种独特的葡萄，它看上去像绿色辣椒，但味道却很甜。

园中所有的葡萄都细心地包裹在纸袋子中，以防止昆虫和鸟类的破坏，因此也无须用到农药。

但在参观这个葡萄园的时候，我心想为什么没有在市场上看到过这些优质的葡萄呢，为什么中国要从智利或美国进口一些低品质的葡萄？答案很简单：中国市场对国产葡萄的品质没信心。

在上海市里，我唯一能找到的国产葡萄是一种个大不甜的品种，厚厚的皮让人看着就没有什么食欲。在欧洲我们也有同样的问题，例如在法国，由于贸易配额限制的关系，超市从国外进口葡萄，而国内又生产太多的葡萄，剩下的只能放着腐烂，等着被扔掉。

马陆最老的葡萄园有 30 多年历史。在这里，我遇到一个农民，他告诉我们他们已经连续三代人都在种植葡萄。现在葡萄种植业发展得越来越好，这激励了下一代农民继续投身葡萄园的工作。当地政府没有让地产商开发葡萄园的地，把地留给果农去发展葡萄种植。这也许在某种程度上是一个很好的政府支持农业发展例子。

离开葡萄园之前，我了解到他们会把葡萄叶用作蔬菜，加入鸡蛋做成美味的菜肴。受到启发，我也设计了一个葡萄园风格的炒蛋卷菜式。

Recipe 2
食谱 2

mallus vineyard scramble egg roll
马陆葡萄园炒蛋卷

4 Servings

4 人份

Ingredients
配料

12	Eggs 鸡蛋
A dash/ 少许	Soy sauce 酱油
A few drops/ 几滴	Grape seed oil 葡萄籽油
100 g	Fresh grape leaves 新鲜葡萄叶
10 g	Garlic fresh 新鲜大蒜
10 g	Chili 辣椒

I use the Toragashi chili powder from Japan. You can also use the French espelette chili pepper which is less spicy but has stronger flavors
我使用日本的七味辣椒粉，或者你可以选择法国的艾斯佩莱特辣椒，味道没那么强烈，但味道很丰富。

Directions
作法

1. Blanch the leaves in the salted water. Cool them down.

在盐水里把叶子灼熟后冷却。

2. Cook the eggs in the bainmarie (a pot with a smaller metal bowl on top that can be used to whisk eggs above the boiling water). Cook slowly; add at the end the thinly chopped chili and a dash of soy sauce.

把鸡蛋放入双层蒸锅（下层装水煮沸，上层有用来煮食物的金属碗，你就可以一边煮一边在碗里搅拌鸡蛋）中慢煮，最后加入薄切的辣椒和少许酱油。

3. Spread the leaves on the clean film and pour the scramble eggs on it; Make a very thick roll.

把叶子撒在干净的保鲜膜上，倒入炒蛋，卷成相当厚实的蛋卷。

4. Put the roll into the boiling water to get make it firm. Take it out and put it in the ice water.

把这条肠状的蛋卷放在沸水中使其牢固，然后放入冰水中。

5. Before serving, add some Chinese pancake on the side. You can serve them cold or hot.

可以上菜了，放些中式煎饼在一旁，可冷食或热食。

Your notes

Great recipes are not created, but perfected.
好的食谱来自一次又一次的修改完善。

Note down the changes you make on this recipe to create your very own version of it.
记录下你对这个食谱做的修改，探寻属于你自己的味道。

Chef's tips
厨师贴士

In buying eggs, whether they are organic or not doesn't really matter much. The media and the market like to promote the advantage of organic food but for eggs, the most important thing is you need to make sure they are fresh. You should check the production date on the packaging. You don't want any eggs that are more than 4 days old.

老实说，其实鸡蛋是否有机并没那么重要。媒体和市场总是宣称有机产品的好处，但对于鸡蛋来说，真正重要的是产品的新鲜度。你需要认真看鸡蛋表面或者外包装上的生产日期，最好的时限是在 4 天以内，超过 4 天的鸡蛋就不敢保证有多新鲜了。

3

故事三

The Organic Vegetables

有机蔬菜

As I have mentioned it before, when I arrived in China with the idea of developing a sustainable organic hotel in downtown Shanghai, everyone thought I was crazy. But I have no doubt that it would work because I have worked with organic products for more than 10 years. It is worth mentioning that at that time Shanghai was in a huge environmental change welcoming the World Expo with the famous campaign "Better City Better Life". From where most westerners stood at the time, that slogan was not much short of a joke.

Shanghai didn't wait till 2010 to start an ecological cleaning process to clear up its polluted environment. 15 years ago, the Chinese government has decided to keep a safe land for the generations to come by keeping the pace of economic development with the effort of protecting the environment, which is why Shanghai spends 18 billion dollars every year in environmental protection. The number is three times that of the French government budget.

The green trend in Shanghai welcoming the World Expo inspired me to do something similar on my side. I decided to visit the farms around shanghai to search for high quality local produce to be exclusively used in my hotel. During my trips, I met at least 50 farmers, some of whom were really passionate about what they were doing. For example, Shanghai Organic who employs at least 250 farmers in the north of Shanghai grows seasonal produce only. The origin of the Shanghai Organic project can be traced back to a German who brought his skills to develop an organic farm in Shanghai. The farm is big like the Central Park in Manhattan, just to give you an idea of the farm scale.

正如我之前所提到的一样，当我来中国的时候，我想在上海市中心开一个可持续有机生态酒店。绝大多数的人认为这样的想法天马行空，脱离现实。但我从一开始就坚信，有机生态酒店肯定在上海行得通。我对有机产品有足够的了解和信心，因为我与有机产品打交道已经超过 10 年了。

值得一提的是，为迎接世博会，上海市提出了“城市，让生活更美好”的口号，当时的上海正处在一个大规模的环境改善行动中。但是，在大多数西方人看来，这个口号不过是个笑话。上海并没有等到 2010 年才开始着手生态净化和治理环境污染。15 年前，中国政府已决心采取有力措施，为中华民族子孙后代留下一片净土繁衍后代，坚持在保持经济发展的同时，做出保护环境的努力。因此上海每年在环保上投入 180 亿美元——这一数字是法国环保预算的三倍。

受上海迎世博环保生态潮流影响，我决定身体力行，做些与环保相关的事。我拜访上海周边的农场，寻找高质量的本地农产品，为我的酒店找到可靠的供应商。拜访期间，我见了五十多个农民，其中不乏对有机农业充满了热情的年轻人。其中，“上海有机项目”就做得特别出色，他们位于上海的北部，雇佣了将近 250 个农民，生产应季农产品。这个项目由一个德国人发起，他热衷于传播有机农业技术，因而在上海开了一个有机农场，占地面积几乎相当于曼哈顿中央公园的大小。

On track to go organic

走上有机的道路

The other farm that caught my attention was the Bio-farm in Pudong, inspired by the ambiance of the Sixties Hippies spirit of peace and love. Three years ago I met a lady named Jane to learn more about her incredible Bio-farm project. The project originally came into being 7 years ago by a Taiwanese American lady who hired some volunteers to support this colossal idea. Several years later Jane was hired to take care of the project. Now we can see over 120 types of fruits, vegetable, and flowers, organic eggs, and naturally raised chickens. There are also a shop and a kitchen to develop recipes, along with a teaching space to educate the young people. The space reaches 100 acres.

Bio-farm is not the only one that is blooming. Many other farms are on track to contribute to the great green trend, striving to leave the best heritage for the nation's future generations.

Not all the farmers I met are the real sense of farmers. The ones who sale the produce "door to door" usually are not those who actually work in the farms. Some of the farms that refused my visit mostly have no idea what are really selling to the market. To the best of my knowledge, organic is not more expensive than regular products. Just not too long ago in China the organic produce was nothing more than a joke to many consumers. With better government regulations and standard controls in product labeled as organic, people's faith in organic product is growing. Now the government is using tracking batch number to track the products from the farm to the consumers. Every new batch must have a code that can be tracked. The organic market does not work on mere faith alone but on better regulations.

另一个给我留下了深刻印象的项目是浦东的"生态农场"，这是一片洋溢着六十年代嬉皮士和平与爱之精神的乐土。三年前，我遇见一位叫"Jane"的女士，她向我介绍了这个项目的历程。这个农场项目诞生于 7 年前，最初是由一位台湾籍美国女士组织了一些志愿者来启动的。几年后，Jane 受聘负责这个项目。现在，这个农场里我们看到超过 120 种水果、蔬菜、鲜花、有机鸡蛋和放养的鸡。这里也有一家商店，一个开发食谱的厨房和一个向年轻人讲解生态农场的教学空间。农场总占地大小达 100 英亩。

这个生态农场并非一枝独秀。其他许多农场也与它一并，为支持绿色潮流，为创造美丽生活，造福子孙后代正在努力着。

并非所有我见到的农民都是真正意义上的农民，通常那些挨家挨户推销生态农产品的人甚至都没有在农场里工作过。我也发现有不少拒绝让我参观的农场对他们自己卖的产品根本一无所知。据我所知，有机产品并不比普通产品更贵。就在不久前，对许多中国消费者而言，中国的有机农产品简直就是一个笑话。但随着对有机农产品的监管和质检更加完善，人们对有机产品的信任度也在日趋上升。如今，政府在实施有机产品批次号跟踪，开始追踪产品从农场到消费者手中的整个过程。每批新产品，都必须配有一个可跟踪的代码。有机产品市场秩序的建立不仅需要买卖双方的诚信度支持，同时也依赖于政府的规范机制。

Recipe 3
食谱 3

virgin oil pesto bio salad
配初榨油香蒜酱有机沙拉

。

4 Servings

4 人份

Pickles recipe
腌菜食谱

100 g ---------- Cauliflower[1] 花椰菜头[1]

100 g ---------- Carrots[2] 胡萝卜[2]

2 ---------- Sprigs fresh dill 新鲜刁草枝

2 ---------- Sprigs cilantro 香菜枝

30 g ---------- Cloves garlic[3] 蒜瓣[3]

2 ---------- Chilies pepper[4] 辣椒[4]

50 g ---------- Green pepper[5] 青椒[5]

1 L ---------- White wine vinegar 白酒醋

6 g ---------- Sea salt 海盐

3 g ---------- Dry mustard 干芥菜

3 g ---------- Ground cumin 孜然粉

2 g ---------- Turmeric 姜黄粉

Organic Salad
有机沙拉

50 g ---------- Green asparagus shaving 绿芦笋屑

50 g ---------- Golden baby beetroot steam 金黄嫩甜菜根

50 g ---------- Heirloom baby carrots shaving 胡萝卜仔屑

50 g ---------- Parsnips shaving 防风草屑

50 g ---------- Fresh wasabi root 新鲜山葵根

Pesto
香蒜酱

100 g ---------- Green zucchini 绿节瓜

30 g ---------- Pine nuts 松仁

20 g ---------- Fresh basil 新鲜罗勒

5 g ---------- Garlic 大蒜

Salt and black pepper 盐和黑胡椒

Beetroot juice
甜菜根汁

1 L ---------- Beetroot juice 甜菜根汁

50 g ---------- Glucose 葡萄糖

Garnish
装饰

10 g ---------- Toasted hazelnuts 烤榛子

1. Broken into florets 切成小朵 2. Peeled, thinly sliced (1 mm in thickness) 去皮，薄切（厚度 1 毫米） 3. Quartered 四等份
4. Quartered lengthwise 纵向四等份 5. Halved 对半

Directions
作法

1. Pickles:

a. Arrange cauliflower and carrots in four half-pint canning jars; set aside.

b. Heat remaining ingredients to a boil in a saucepan over medium heat, cook for 10 minutes.

c. Turn off the heat; sit for 5 minutes.

d. Pour the mixture over the vegetables to cover.

e. Cover jars tightly; cool to room temperature, about 1 hour.

f. Refrigerate at least for three days before serving. You can keep them a year in the fridge.

腌菜：a. 把花椰菜和胡萝卜放入 4 个半品脱容量的罐头瓶里，放在一旁准备好。

b. 把剩下的原料放入炖锅中用中火加热至沸腾，煮大约 10 分钟。

c. 关掉火，让其浸泡 5 分钟。

d. 把混合物淋在蔬菜上面。

e. 把瓶子盖紧，冷却至室温，大约 1 小时。

f. 使用前冷藏至少 3 天。你可以在冰箱里保存 1 年。

2. Pesto:

a. Chop the zucchini in big chunks and boil it for 10 minutes in water.

b. Drain and put them in cool water.

c. Blend the zucchini with the pine nuts, basil and the garlic.

d. Add the seasoning.

香蒜酱：a. 把节瓜切成大块，放入水中煮 10 分钟。

b. 沥干并使其冷却。

c. 把节瓜、松仁、罗勒和大蒜放入搅拌机中搅拌。

e. 加入调味料。

3. Make the beetroot juice:

Extract the juice and pour it in the pot and add the glucose; boil it until you get a thick texture.

甜菜根汁作法：榨取甜菜汁，倒入罐中，放入葡萄糖，煮至沸腾变稠。

4. Set up:

Brush the plate with the beetroot juice; season the leaves with the dressing; add the drops of pesto on the plate, the hazelnuts, and the leaves on top of the juice, along with the shaving veggies.

摆设：用甜菜汁水涂抹盘子，在甜菜叶子上淋上汁液。放入几滴香蒜酱到盘子中，然后放入榛子，叶子浇上汁，再放入蔬菜碎。

Your notes

Great recipes are not created, but perfected.
好的食谱来自一次又一次的修改完善。

Note down the changes you make on this recipe to create your very own version of it.
记录下你对这个食谱做的修改，探寻属于你自己的味道。

Chef's tips
厨师贴士

To choose my vegetables I always touch them to check if they are firm enough but not too hard to touch. I would check the green stem of the zucchini to see if it is bright green to make sure they are fresh. Never buy the pre peeled vegetable or fruits because there usually are not fresh.

选择蔬菜的时候，我经常会选择动手去触摸看是它否有弹性，同时又不能太硬。我会检查节瓜的绿茎，它必须是翠绿色的，因此判断它是否新鲜。千万别买已经削皮的瓜果，因为它们通常都不新鲜。

4

故事四

The Organic Mushroom Farm

有机蘑菇农场

I met an amazing family, the Peng family, owner of the Fengfu Company doing the edible mushroom cultivation business. Founded by Mr.Peng Zhaowang, Fengfu Company is the first mushroom logs supplier. It pioneered the management model of mushroom logs for farms. For many years, its products, facilities, and the solution plans have helped their clients globally establish and develop their own mushroom farms.

The Peng family were not expecting us on the day when we visited the company, yet from what I saw, their equipment is new and extremely clean. I have to say I was really impressed by their professionalism. The company has a long history of 47 years in this particular industry. The whole family is very well organized and together they created the system of cultivating mushrooms through the log planting technology. They have so far cultivated 12 types of unique mushrooms that originally were from the wild forests in China's Yunnan Province.

丰福公司，一家从事食用菌栽培的公司，我见到了一户了不起的彭氏人家。丰福公司由彭兆旺先生创办，是第一家食用菌菌棒供应商，而且还开创了食用菌菌棒农场的经营模式。多年来，对于世界各地那些想创立发展自己蘑菇农场的客户而言，丰福公司的产品、设备、解决方案一直是最可靠的选择，依靠它很多人实现了建立自己蘑菇种植场的愿望。

拜访之前，他们并不知道我们会那一天来，但是我很惊喜地发现他们设备崭新，整个环境一尘不染。我不得不说，他们的专业精神很值得称赞。这家公司在蘑菇领域已经有 47 年的历史了，彭家团结一致，创建了菌棒种植技术培育蘑菇的系统。他们至今已培育了十二种来自中国云南野生森林的独特蘑菇。

Mushrooms and its Chinese Flavor

蘑菇的中国风味

Mushrooms have been considered in numerous civilizations the food of gods that is blessed with the gift of immortality. The first cultivation of mushroom could be traced back to 4500 years ago. It's the Parisian who developed the modern techniques of cultivating mushroom in the 1650s. The famous Paris mushroom grows in the caves near Paris. To me, mushrooms have a strong Chinese flavor, given that the country produces about half of all cultivated mushrooms, boasting that it has the world's largest variety of mushrooms. As the world's largest edible mushroom producer, China has a mushroom market valued at 30 billion US dollars. Almost all the dry mushrooms used in cooking are from China.

Yet, many years the mushroom farms in China have been involved in pesticide pollution scandals. It's important to note that mushrooms absorb toxins easily like a sponge which has compelled mushrooms farms to promote environmental protection to help guarantee green products up to food safety standards.

许多古老文明相信蘑菇是神的食物，人吃了可以长生不老。最早的蘑菇的培育可追溯到 4500 年前而现代蘑菇培育方法则由巴黎人于 1650 年发明。著名的巴黎蘑菇一般生长在巴黎市附近的洞穴中。对我而言，蘑菇洋溢着一股浓郁的中国风味：中国有全世界最丰富的蘑菇品种，生产的蘑菇总量占世界人工培育蘑菇的一半。作为全球最大的食用菌生产商，中国蘑菇市场价值达 300 亿美元，全世界烹饪使用的干蘑菇几乎都来自于中国。

然而，中国的蘑菇农场多年来多次曝出农药污染的丑闻。值得注意，蘑菇可以像海绵一样容易吸收环境中的毒素，这在一定程度上也迫使蘑菇农场增强环境保护意识，确保按照食品安全标准生产绿色食品。

pudong organic mushroom tea

浦东有机蘑菇茶

20 Servings

20 人份

Vegetables broth
蔬菜汤

6 kg	White mushrooms quarters	四分切的白蘑菇
3 kg	Minced shallots	葱头碎
3 kg	Minced fennels	茴香碎
100 g	Olive oil	橄榄油
400 g	Butter	黄油
1 kg	Dry mushrooms powder	干蘑菇粉

Mushrooms Tea
蘑菇茶

4 kg	Fresh mushrooms quarters[1]	四分切鲜蘑菇[1]
1 kg	Minced leek	大葱碎
1 kg	Dry black fungus	干木耳
200 pcs	Regliss	甘草
10 L	Vegetables broth	蔬菜汤

Garnish
装饰

1.5 kg	Dry mushrooms slices	干蘑菇片

1. Enoki, shiitake, white mushrooms 金针菇、香菇、白蘑菇

Directions
作法

1. Vegetables Broth:

a. Sauté the white mushrooms with butter and olive oil. Add a little bit of salt.

b. Cook until the mushrooms become brown color; add the shallots, fennel and cook for 3 minutes.

c. Add water, just enough to cover the mushrooms.

d. Add salt and the mushrooms powder. Simmer and cook with a lid for 30 minutes.

蔬菜浓汤：a. 用黄油和橄榄油炒白蘑菇，放入少许盐。

b. 炒至蘑菇变成棕色，放入大葱，茴香，再煮 3 分钟。

c. 放入水，刚好没过蘑菇。

d. 放入盐和蘑菇粉，盖上盖子焖煮 30 分钟。

2. Mushrooms Tea:

a. Sauté the white mushrooms with olive oil. Add the leek. Wait for it to turn a light brown color.

b. Deglaze with water. Repeat for 3 times.

c. Add the vegetables broth, add the dry mushrooms and cook slowly for 4 hours.

d. Add the regliss before serving.

蘑菇茶：a. 用橄榄油炒白蘑菇，加入大葱，着浅棕色。

b. 用水去渣，重复 3 次。

c. 放入蔬菜汤，加入干蘑菇，慢煮 4 小时。

d. 最后上菜前加入甘草。

3. Set up:

You can serve the tea in a tea pot. Garnish the dish with dry mushrooms or raw fresh mushrooms.

摆盘：茶可以用茶壶上，放些干蘑菇和作为装饰的新鲜生蘑菇在汤碗旁。

Your notes

Great recipes are not created, but perfected.
好的食谱来自一次又一次的修改完善。

Note down the changes you make on this recipe to create your very own version of it.
记录下你对这个食谱做的修改，探寻属于你自己的味道。

Chef's tips
厨师贴士

The used chopped mushrooms in this recipe can be used to make broth, a pie or even samosa or mushroom spring rolls.

当你完成这个食谱，你不需要把所有切碎的蘑菇放入垃圾筒，你可以用来做汤，做派，做萨莫萨三角饺或者是做蘑菇春卷。

5

故事五

Yangcheng Lake, the Hairy crab, wild eel and more

阳澄湖，大闸蟹，野生鳗鱼…

There is something unique about Yangcheng Lake during its low season from November to August of the next year. At this time of the year it's the heaven on earth for seafood gourmets from China or from the West. Before I arrived at the lake, I went through several small villages by the rivers, enjoying the refreshing views of the water ponds, rice fields and other vegetable fields. It is a real ecological paradise which is only 80 kilometers from downtown Shanghai. I felt like I was back to the old China when nature ruled and before modernization took over this ancient nation. The clear water, birds, a wide range of aquatic plants, fish, shrimps, frogs, crayfish, and shellfish...together made up my impression of this lake area that is known for its hairy crabs.

The hairy crab, or Mitten crab, is a unique species in Asia, specially Korea and China. But the best ones come from Yangcheng Lake. The sales of this crab officially start from mid-September and lasts for two to three months. The Chinese authorities have set up some specific name tags to crack down on counterfeit.

淡季的澄阳湖是一个独特的地方。

在上海的中国人或是外国人都知道它是吃海鲜美食的好地方。

沿着河边，穿过几个小村庄，一路享受着水塘，稻田，菜地的田园风光，不知不觉，阳澄湖到了。这个距离上海市区仅 80 公里的生态乐园很让人惊喜。

阳澄湖车不多，安静、清新，充满自然野性。对我而言，它又是一个对传统中国的回眸之所。站在湖边，我仿佛回到了几个世纪之前的中国，享受那个时代所崇尚的人与自然的和谐。视野所及处，水波清澈，百鸟争鸣，色调各异的水生植物、鱼、青蛙、小龙虾、虾、贝壳齐聚一起。

毛蟹也叫中华绒螯蟹，亚洲特有的一种蟹，主要分布在中国、韩国。但最好的毛蟹产自阳澄湖。它的销售期是从 9 月中旬后的两三个月。为避免假的阳澄湖蟹泛滥市场，中国政府在蟹产品的标签使用上有明确的规定。

The one-of-a-kind hairy crabs

独一无二的毛蟹

Some farmers would buy crabs from other places and have no qualms about claiming that they are from Yangcheng Lake. In France oysters dealers play a similar game in the peak season. It's not easy buying authentic Yangcheng Lake Crabs. On this trip I was lucky enough to have the chance to try the real thing since at that time all other crabs were out of season.

The hairy crab is maximally 10 cm in diameters with its claws covering with dark hairs. Normally for this type of crabs, the maturation period is 5 years, but in China they can start selling them after 2 years. Hairy crab has a remarkable resistance to polluted environment. All of these together make it the most expensive crabs in China, about 100 USD a kilo.

Why is Yangcheng Lake so special? This area has been protected for many years by the Chinese authorities, keeping it away from garbage, heavy metal and pesticide pollution. To me it was weird to see a lake without a boat, yet, thank to that, we can enjoy a wide variety of aquatic products.

有一些农民会购买一些其他地方产的螃蟹来冒充阳澄湖大闸蟹。法国牡蛎生产商也有如出一辙的戏法。采捞牡蛎的时节，他们总免不了会从其他地方调来些牡蛎，冒充法国生产。所以不仅中国存在这个现象，在其他很多国家也会出现类似的问题。这次我很幸运能品尝到了真正的阳澄湖大闸蟹，因为我去的时候其它品种的蟹已经过季下市了。

最大的毛蟹可达 10 厘米宽，爪子上覆盖着黑毛。毛蟹要生长 5 年才成熟，但在中国，2 年的毛蟹就可以销售了。这种蟹还有一个特性，它即使在污染的环境中一样容易存活。各种品性合加使得阳澄湖大闸蟹成为中国最贵的蟹，每公斤高达 100 美元。

为什么阳澄湖的蟹特别好呢？因为阳澄湖地区几乎完全被中国政府保护了起来，连续多年没有垃圾、重金属和农药的污染。站在湖边放眼望去，没有船的湖面一片宁静，可以轻易看到湖中的其他水生物。

Steps in preparing Hairy Crabs

Note that fishermen catch the crabs with complete precaution.

-Brush it all over to thoroughly remove the mud and the seaweed.

-Rinse it.

-Tie the claws up with a string, which is not as easy as it may seem to be. I tried and it was not easy at all.

-After that do the last cleaning.

Then the hairy crab is ready for cooking.

准备烹饪大闸蟹的小技巧：

渔民在捕捞它时要做好十足的防护措施。

—刷蟹去除全部污泥或小海藻。

—冲洗。

—用麻线把蟹脚和钳子扎紧（这是看着容易，做着难的功夫，我自己试过，这活儿一点也不容易）。

—这之后，再洗一次。

这样毛蟹就可以用来做菜了。

yangcheng lake hairy crab variations

玩转阳澄湖大闸蟹

Nem stick
能母条

100 g ---------- River White fish 河白鱼
8 cl ---------- Cream 奶油
1 ---------- Egg 鸡蛋
100 g ---------- Hairy crab meat 大闸蟹肉
5 g ---------- Urchin raw 生海胆
5 leaves ---------- Chinese parsley 香菜
5 leaves ---------- Fresh mint 新鲜薄荷
Seasoning 调味料
4 ---------- Spring roll dough sheet 春卷面皮

Make a long and thin nem stick (20 cm long and 1 cm wide)
制成又长又薄的能母条 (20 厘米长，1 厘米宽）

Steamed Hairy crab
整大闸蟹

4 ---------- Hairy crab[1] 大闸蟹[1]
10 ml ---------- Shanxi vinegar 山西醋
Salted water for boiling 煮沸的盐水
Cracker cracked green pepper 绿胡椒碎

Hairy crab soup
大闸蟹汤

4 ---------- Hairy crab shell[2] 大闸蟹壳[2]
50 g ---------- Chinese cabbage 大白菜
100 g ---------- River Fish bones 河鱼鱼骨
A dash ---------- Soy sauce 酱油
5 g ---------- Galanga root 南姜根

Crab shell salt
蟹壳盐

Crab shell 蟹壳
10 g ---------- Flake salt 盐花

1. Without the claws. 只是蟹身，无需蟹钳
2. Claws/body parts 钳和身体部分

Directions
作法

1. Nem sticks:

a. Blend all the ingredients, and then mesh the mix to make it as thin as possible and easy to spread.

b. Spread the mix on the spring roll sheet and use a bamboo skewer to roll it (the diameter must be less than 1 cm).

c. Put them in the freezer before you fry them.

能母条：a. 把所有的原材料搅拌在一起，用滤网过滤混合物至非常细薄，以方便涂抹。

b. 把混合物涂抹在春卷皮上，使用直径必须小于 1 厘米的竹叉来卷。

c. 先冰冻，再煎炸。

2. Steam the hairy crabs:

a. Steam the crabs for 2 minutes.

b. Remove all the legs (to be used for the soup); keep only the body.

c. Open the body and remove the lung and the stomach (keep the stomach); remove the meat and keep it plain.

d. Blend the stomach with a few drops of vinegar and add the pepper. Mesh.

e. Put the plain meat back inside and the stomach sauce on top. Serve warm.

蒸大闸蟹：a. 将蟹清蒸两分钟。

b. 去除所有的腿（用于做汤），只留蟹身。

c. 打开蟹身，去除肺和胃（留着胃备用），为保持原味，取出蟹肉。

d. 加入几滴醋把蟹胃搅拌好，加入胡椒，过滤。

e. 将蟹肉装进蟹壳，浇上蟹胃汁，趁热上菜。

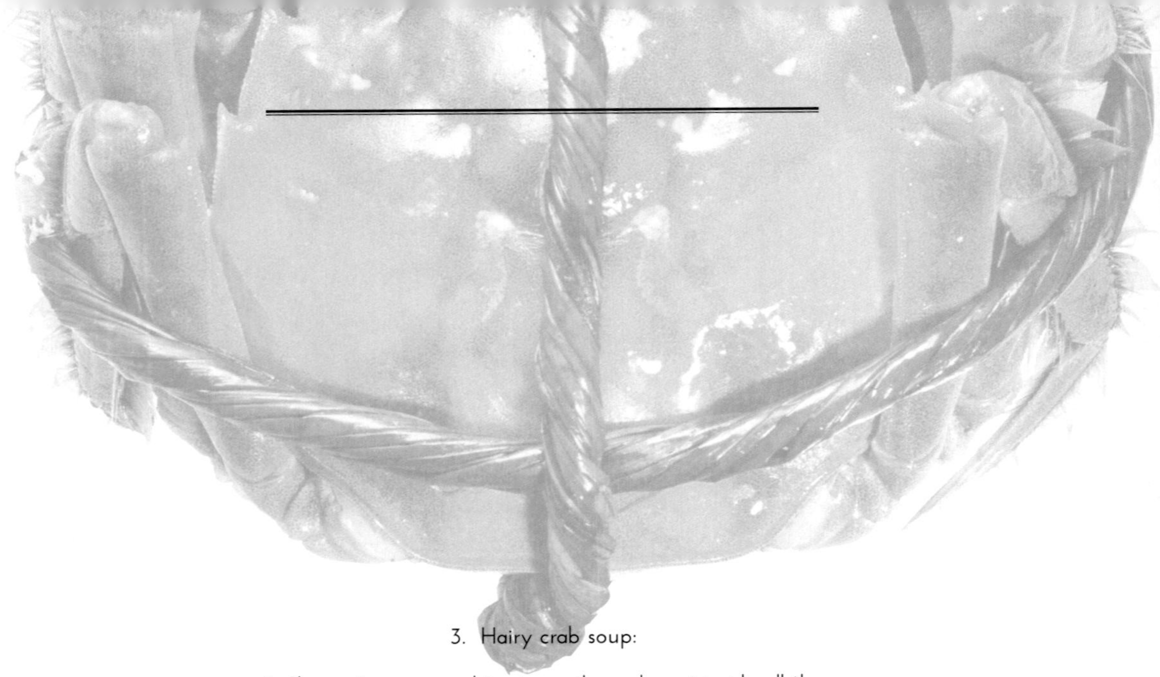

3. Hairy crab soup:

In the water you used to steam the crab, put inside all the shell left over, add the cabbage, the chopped galangal and few drops of soy sauce. Keep boiling for 2 hours. Drain the broth and use a fabric to filter.

大闸蟹汤：把所有剩下的蟹壳放进你刚才用来蒸蟹的水里，再放入大白菜，切碎的南姜和几滴酱油。煮沸 2 小时，用布滤去汤汁。

4. Crab shell salt:

Dry all the shell for a whole night to get them very dry; use a blender to get a thin powder and then use a mesh to remove all the big pieces. Add the flake salt.

蟹壳盐：把蟹壳晾置风干一晚，使其足够干。使用搅拌器制成粉，用滤网除去大颗的粒，加入盐花。

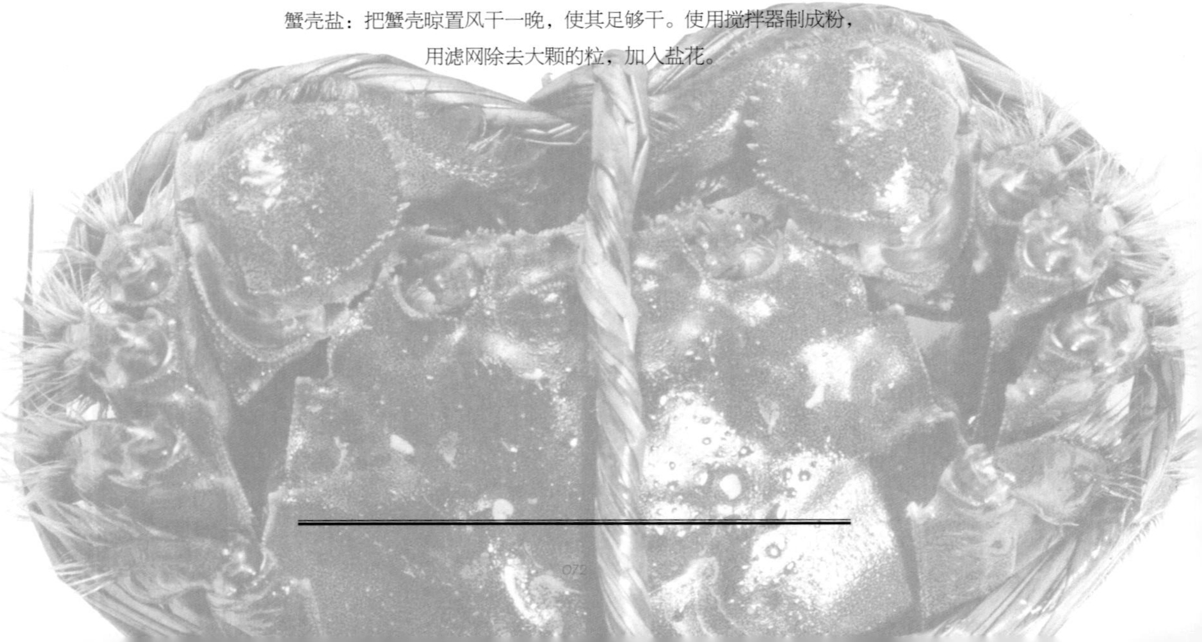

Your notes

Great recipes are not created, but perfected.
好的食谱来自一次又一次的修改完善。

Note down the changes you make on this recipe to create your very own version of it.
记录下你对这个食谱做的修改，探寻属于你自己的味道。

Chef's tips:
厨师贴士

Usually it's better to choose the female crabs in China or Europe. Generally the female crabs in China are more expensive. For the soup you can use the male ones while for the steaming, pick the female ones. When you boil the hairy crab or any other seafood it's better to use the water from a fish tank or the river or the sea to enhance the taste of seafood. To undercook seafood can keep a juicy texture and a better flavor.

无论在中国还是欧洲，通常人们都会选择母蟹。在中国，母蟹更贵，可以用来蒸煮，而公蟹可做汤。当你烹饪蟹或者其他海鲜时，最好选用鱼塘，河流或大海这些可提鲜的水源，这样可以保持海鲜的原汁原味。

6

故事六

Fengjing Water Town, Jinshan County

金山县，枫泾水城

Located in the southwest of Shanghai, Fengjing Ancient Town is 57 kilometers from Shanghai City, it has long been known as a typical ancient water town, as well as one of the four most famous towns in the south China. Other towns that enjoy similar reputations are Nanxun Ancient Town, Wangjiangjing in Zhejiang Province, and Shengze in Jiangsu Province.

Fengjing Ancient Town has a history of over 1,500 years. Demarcated by the boundary river in its center, the beautiful small town was governed separately by Zhejiang and Jiangsu Provinces from 1430 during the Ming Dynasty (1368-1644).

The first thing I noticed of this water town was not its waters but its buildings which were built in the Ming and Qing dynasty style. The buildings were mostly low-rise with specific architectural styles described in City Village. For me it's not a village I expected to find. To reach each part of the town you can use the 52 bridges across the water network.

When you are there by the water you would feel like the time has stopped for several centuries. With the tranquility and peace of this this delicate town the bubbling of downtown Shanghai feels like thousands of kilometers away. The sweet nature of the local was a plus to the enjoyment of the stay. They were always happy to take care of anything I needed.

The local Chinese culture and the history portrayed quite a different image of the Chinese metropolis.

位于上海的西南，距离上海市 57 公里的枫泾古镇是一个典型的中国水乡古镇。它是中国南方四大著名古镇之一，另外三个分别是浙江的南浔古镇、王江泾以及江苏的盛泽。

枫泾古镇有 1500 多年的历史。划定边界的河流从古镇中心穿过，这个漂亮的小镇从明朝（1368 – 1644）的 1430 年起就由浙江和江苏两省分别治理。

虽是水乡，但进去后这个地方最吸引眼球的并不是水，而是许多明清风格的建筑。楼层低矮，却有着十分独特的建筑风格，恰如你在《城市村庄》中所见到的。对我，这个村庄实在有点出乎意料。包括 52 座桥梁与纵横的水路网络（小运河），可抵达枫泾水城任何一个地方。

站在水边，时间仿佛已经停止了几个世纪。这个小县城的平和安宁能让人暂时遗忘上海的喧闹街区。当地人的乐于助人和好客性情也让游玩更加愉快。我记得当时我有任何需要帮助的地方当地人都热心帮忙。本地特有的中国文化味和历史味让枫泾古镇呈现出上海这个中国大都市不一样的一面。

A taste of the water town flavor

水乡风味

The water town is also known for its local delicacies, of which the yellow wine, pork trotter, Zhuang Yuan Cake and Tian Xiang Dry Bean Curd are known as the "Four Treasures of Fengjing". I found in the street the most special dish, the smoked wild frog legs. In Europe we don't usually eat frog legs that way. Yet I think the smoking process enhances the aromas of each bite.

To me, one of the most interesting experiences in this town was trying all those handmade street food like pork dragon boat and steam river mussels. The taste was simple but carried a flavor that was matured over time by the local culture.

Here you can find many small restaurants where you can enjoy the traditional local food in private rooms. One impressive dish I remember was the pork trotter marinated in soy sauce, which tasted similar to the Burgundy ham (A piece of ham boiled with fresh herbs) in France.

The other one was the huge crayfishes that tasted so much better than the ones you can get in downtown Shanghai. The taste was a perfect mix of classic Chinese flavor with a dash of Muslim taste with the use of crushed cumin seeds. I talked to the chef who made the dishes who was relaxing at the back of the kitchen but he refused to reveal his secret ingredients in the crayfish dish.

The riverside street food presented a colorful side of a quiet water town. If I am to recommend a place to visit in Shanghai after the Yancheng lake, it will surely be Fengjing water town.

古镇另一大特色是当地的美味佳肴，黄酒、猪蹄、状元糕和天香豆腐干被誉为“枫泾四宝”。我在街上发现一些对老外而言很独特的食物，例如烟熏野生青蛙腿。在欧洲，我们用非常不同的方式吃青蛙。但这里的烟熏青蛙腿很美味，由于烟熏这个特殊步骤，吃起来每一小口都是满口馨香。

我觉得最有趣的经历就是品尝街边小摊上就可轻易购得的本地小吃，例如猪肉龙舟和蒸河蚌等。这些小吃的味道都比较单一，制作方法也相对简单，可细细品尝却能感受到其中古镇熏陶的特殊风味。

在古镇，你可以找到许多小餐厅，你可以在那里的私人包厢中享受当地传统食物。简单却美味的食物，例如有一道猪蹄菜是由酱油汁腌制而成的，味道非常接近法国勃艮第火腿（一种用很多不同香草炖煮的火腿）。另一道给我留下了深刻印象的菜是用大只的小龙虾做的，味道比上海市区能吃到的小龙虾好吃很多。它似乎是中餐和穆斯林风味的完美结合，吃的出是加了穆斯林菜肴常用的孜然。制作这些佳肴的厨师在后台厨房歇息，我和他聊了几句，但是他不愿透露烹制小龙虾的秘方。

街边的小吃给这个宁静之地增添了几分色彩。去完阳澄湖后，如果要选一个上海的地方去继续游玩，我会推荐枫泾水城。

Recipe 6

食谱 6

jinshan smoked frog legs garlic and parsley juice

金山烟熏田鸡腿，配大蒜和蕃茜汁

4 Servings

4 人份

Ingredients
配料

4 dozens/ 打	Wild frog's legs 野生田鸡腿
10 g	Flour 面粉
100 g	Wooden chip 木碎

Puree
果泥

	Garlic purée[1] 大蒜泥[1]
	Parsley juice[2] 蕃茜汁[2]
	Oil for cooking 调和油
50 g	Butter 黄油
little/ 少许	Salt and pepper 盐和胡椒

1. Made with 400 g garlic. 用 400 克的大蒜制成。
2. Made with 200 g parsley. 用 200 克的蕃茜制成。

Directions
作法

1. Garlic purée:

a. Crush the heads of garlic with the palm of your hand to separate the cloves. Immerse them in a saucepan of cold water and boil for 2 minutes. Remove with a strainer. Repeat the process four times; change the water each time.

b. Peel and halve the garlic cloves. Remove the germ in the center with a paring knife.

c. Return the peeled garlic to the saucepan full of cold water and boil for 2 minutes. Repeat the process four times, changing the water each time.

d. Rinse and drain the garlic cloves. Purée in a blender. If the mixture is too thick, thin it with a little milk and blend again.

大蒜泥：a. 把蒜瓣分离，用冷水在锅里浸泡并煮 2 分钟，用过滤器隔开，重复该步骤 4 次，每次都要换水。

b. 把蒜瓣去皮并切半，把中间的胚芽用厨师刀去掉。

c. 把去完皮的大蒜放回装满冷水的锅里煮 2 分钟，重复该步骤 4 次，每次都需要更换水。

d. 冲洗并沥干蒜瓣，用搅拌机打成泥。如果太稠了，用少许牛奶再搅拌一次来稀释。

2. The parsley juice:

a. Wash and drain the parsley. Cook it in boiling salted water for 4-5 minutes, then refresh in cold water.

b. Drain well in a strainer, then purée in the blender. Thin with a little water to obtain the consistency of a coulis. Set aside.

蕃茜汁：a. 清洗并沥干蕃茜，在沸腾的盐水中煮 4–5 分钟，然后放入冷水中。

b. 用滤网沥干，然后放入搅拌机里打成泥，用少许水来稀释，使稠度一致。放好备用。

3. The frog's legs:

a. Cut off the ends of the legs and remove the two bottom muscles, leaving only the upper muscle.

b. Put them in a metal bowl with a grill underneath. Place the wooden chips underneath the bowl and light them up. Cover the bowl and leave them overnight to create a strong smoke flavor.

c. Cook the frog's legs.

d. Season the frog's legs with salt and pepper. Flour them. Prepare a plate topped with 4 sheets of paper towel.

e. Heat the garlic purée and parsley juice separately in two small sauce pans set over low heat.

f. In a skillet, heat 1 tbsp. oil, then add the butter. When it is foamy, add the frog's legs. Brown them on one side for 1 minute, turn them, reduce the heat to medium, and cook 2-3 minutes longer depending on the size. Drain and place on the paper towels.

田鸡腿：a. 切掉腿部的末端，去除两边底部的肌肉，留下上面的肌肉。

b. 把其放入金属碗中，碗下放一个烤架，烤架下放木碎。把木碎点燃，盖上碗，让其隔夜，需要有浓烈烟熏的口味。

c. 把田鸡腿煮熟。

d. 用盐和胡椒调味，裹上面粉，准备一个放上 4 张纸巾的盘子。

e. 分别用 2 个小锅小火加热大蒜泥和蕃茜汁。

f. 用一长柄煎锅加热 1 汤匙的油，然后放入黄油。当起泡后，放入田鸡腿。煎一面 1 分钟至棕褐色，翻转，转中火，根据大小煮多 2 到 3 分钟，沥干后放在纸巾上。

4. Set up:

Pour the parley jus on the bottom; put the frogs and then some garlic puree.

摆盘：把蕃茜汁倒到底部，放入田鸡，然后再放大蒜泥。

Your notes

Great recipes are not created, but perfected.
好的食谱来自一次又一次的修改完善。

Note down the changes you make on this recipe to create your very own version of it.
记录下你对这个食谱做的修改，探寻属于你自己的味道。

Chef's tips:
厨师贴士

In china most of time people use the bullfrogs but I choose smaller frogs whose meat is juicier and tenderer. If you buy fresh frogs' legs, it's better to use them on the second day so the meat would taste tenderer.

在中国，通常人们采用牛蛙来烹饪，但我会选择体积相对小的田鸡，因为它的肉更多汁，更柔软。如果你买的田鸡腿非常新鲜，最好留到第二天使用，这样它的肉质会更加柔软。

7

故事七

Chongming Island

崇明岛

Many Shanghainese never set foot on this Island Paradise.

In China, numerous people frequent Hainan, but Chongming Island is outside their realm of experience. This is an unfortunate fact as Chongming is the largest alluvial island in the world, as well as the first worldwide eco-system project - commenced in 2007.

To reach this destination, you must cross a huge bridge over the Yangtze river, a vast expanse of water, wind generators on the banks, oil factories and gigantic cargo ships carrying containers.

Up to this point there is little visible that is wild, green and organic. Rather, a vast industrial network boasts of China's economic prowess to everyone who crosses this river. Only as you approach the island's coast can you truly begin to enjoy this fantastic natural paradise - its tiny villages, the rice, orchards, and fields.

许多上海人从未涉足过这个天堂之岛。

在中国，许多人会去海南度假，去崇明岛的人却不多。这样一片美丽的土地就这样被忽略了。崇明岛是世界上最大的冲积岛，在 2007 年，全球第一个世界级的生态系统项目就是在崇明岛启动的。

前往崇明岛，必须跨越长江上一座雄伟的大桥，途经一片广阔水域，沿途可以看到岸边的风力发动机，石油工厂和载着集装箱的大型船舶。这时出现在眼前的仅是一个庞大的工业网，让你在横渡这条河时，感觉到中国经济的强大。只有当你抵达崇明岛海岸附近，你就可以开始享受这美妙的自然天堂一它的小村庄、稻米、果园和田地。

前方施工
800m

Buffalo Milk

水牛奶

On the way to Dongtan Wetland Park, I saw several buffalo grazing near some houses. I never imagined that I would see buffalo just an hour from downtown! So I jumped out of the car to get a closer look and discovered that the owner was making a kind of cheese from his buffaloes' milk. Who knew there are people making fresh cheese in the middle of no-where on this isolated Shanghai island?

Not too long after my Chongming island trip, I met a lady in Pudong who makes mozzarella cheese. She was neither Italian nor Chinese, and at the beginning she had no clue about the cheese business. Her passion for Italian food was what helped her succeed. This lady was Korean, named Kyeong Joo Lee, or simply, "K J".

She lived in Italy for many years with her husband before they moved to Shanghai. Because Shanghai was not her cup of tea, she decided to make something that reminded her of Italy - cheese.

She went back to Italy to look for the necessary machinery and for someone who could train her to make this cheese. After several weeks she obtained the machine and had begun to profit from the experience of a local cheese Artisan. To ensure a quality product, she used imported milk from Germany.

Week after week she got average results. Eventually she sent the cheese master she had hired back to Italy because of financial issues. The miracle began when she met an Italian couple in her building. The husband was a chef at an Italian restaurant in Shanghai. She offered the couple some mozzarella cheese to sample and they gave her feedback on the taste. Gradually she learned how to make the best cheese in Shanghai. Words spread and many other Italian chefs requested the precious "White treasure". It wasn't marketing that brought her success, but the pure passion of one lady on a quest for excellent food.

去东滩湿地公园的路上，我见到几头水牛在村间的房屋边悠然吃草。我从未想过，在离市中心仅一个小时车程的地方可以看见水牛！所以我连忙下车，近看竟发现主人家正在用水牛奶做奶酪。谁能想到在如此偏僻的孤岛上，会有人做新鲜奶酪呢？

崇明岛之行不久后，我又在浦东见到一位做意大利马苏里拉奶酪的女士。这位女士既不是意大利人也不是中国人，刚起步时对奶酪市场一窍不通。她对意大利美食的热情是她取得成功的主要原因。这位女士是韩国人，名叫Kyeong Joo Lee，或简称“K J”。

搬到上海前，她和她丈夫在意大利生活了很多年。刚开始时她不是很喜欢上海的生活，于是她决定做些让她想起意大利美好时光的东西—奶酪。

回到意大利，她开始寻找做奶酪的设备以及教她做奶酪的技师。几个礼拜后，她买到了设备，并从一个当地奶酪技师那儿学得技术。为确保奶酪成品的质量，她只选用从德国进口的牛奶。时间一天一天地过去，她做的奶酪的没什么突破。面对资金成本的压力，她不得不把她请的那位奶酪大师送回了意大利。突然有一天，奇迹发生了，她遇到一对意大利夫妇，丈夫正好是家意大利餐厅的厨师。她给他们一些马苏里拉奶酪做样品，他们给她反馈意见，渐渐地，她做的奶酪越来越好，她学会了如何制作最好的奶酪。她的奶酪有很好的口碑，在上海的诸多意大利厨师纷纷点名要用这种“白色珍品”。她获得成功不是靠过多的营销，而是依靠她对卓越美食的热情和追求。

An important detail: she avoids using the local milk - not for hygienic safety, but because the milk from China, the USA, and Australia cannot be used to make the cheese.

一个重要的细节：她不用本地牛奶做她的芝士一不是出于卫生安全的考虑，仅仅是因为中国、美国和澳大利亚的牛奶都不适合做这种奶酪。

Recipe 7
食谱 7

chongming buffalo milk espuma with creamy carrot and ginger soup
崇明岛水牛奶慕斯配胡萝卜和生姜浓汤

Ingredients
配料

1.5 L ---------- Chicken stock 鸡汤
500 g ---------- Carrot 胡萝卜
200 g ---------- Potato 土豆
500 ml ---------- Milk 鸡汤
50 g ---------- Butter 黄油

Seasonings
调料

20 g ---------- Fresh Parsley 鲜香菜
2 g ---------- Ginger julienne 姜丝
A drizzle of cream 一点奶油
5 ---------- Lavash cumin crackers Lavash 孜然饼干

Espuma
慕斯

200 ml ---------- Milk 牛奶
170 ml ---------- 35% cream 35% 奶油
125 g ---------- Chongming mozzarella 崇明芝士
3 g ---------- xantana powder 黄原胶粉

Garnish
装饰

20 g ---------- Baby carrot shaving 小胡萝卜皮

Directions
作法

1. For the soup:

a. Cook the carrots and potatoes in the chicken stock; drain, reserving the stock.

b. purée the carrots and potatoes in a blender with 500 ml milk.

c. Return everything to a pot with the stock; mix well; season with salt, pepper, ginger julienne and reheat.

d. Serve with butter, a drizzle of cream and a little fresh parsley.

汤：a. 将胡萝卜和土豆在鸡汤中煮熟；过滤汤，保留汤。

b. 把胡萝卜和土豆放入搅拌机，加入 500 毫升牛奶搅拌。

c. 把所有食材放入一个锅中，加入保留的汤；拌匀；加入盐、胡椒和姜丝，重新加热。

d. 配上黄油，一点奶油和新鲜的香菜。

2. For the mozzarella espuma:

a. Boil the milk, add the cream.

b. Add the mozzarella to be melted and strained.

c. Add xantana on top.

马苏里拉奶酪慕斯：a. 煮沸牛奶，然后加入奶油。

b. 加入芝士，待它融化加入黄原胶粉。

Your notes

Great recipes are not created, but perfected.
好的食谱来自一次又一次的修改完善。

Note down the changes you make on this recipe to create your very own version of it.
记录下你对这个食谱做的修改，探寻属于你自己的味道。

Chef's tips:
厨师贴士

For this recipe you can choose any mozzarella, local or imported. You can also use some other cheese like the parmesan cheese but you would need to reduce the salt quantity.

You can make the same recipe without cheese. Use fresh whole milk, with salt and xantana the same amount of the recipe's; put everything in a spray bottle and you will get the same texture but the taste is weaker than the one made with cheese.

这个食谱，你可以选择任何品种的马苏里拉奶酪，本地或进口的都可以。你也可以使用一些其他的奶酪（像帕尔马干酪），但必须用少一点盐。这个配方不用芝士也可以，你可以用新鲜的全脂牛奶，加上盐和黄原胶粉（量和原配方相同）；把所有东西都放在一个喷雾瓶里摇均匀，你会得到和原配方一样的质感，但味道会淡些。

8

故事八

Wild Paradise

野生的天堂

After this stop we went to the Dongtan Wetlands - the glory of Shanghai.

With no noise, fresh air, and a slight wind, Dongtan is a great getaway on weekdays, when no one else is there. The whole place is unique; it's hard to believe that you are near Shanghai. Birds, ponds, lotuses and lakes full of water lilies surround you. You discover diverse landscapes while simply walking across a footbridge.

I did not go there for the birds, however, but for one thing - organic bamboo shoots. A unique bamboo plantation that stood in the center of this huge park provided me with a good supply of bamboo shoot samples to use in one of my dishes.

在这短暂逗留后，我们前往东滩湿地，传说中的“天堂”。

没有噪音，空气新鲜，微风轻拂一工作日去简直棒极了，根本没人在那儿。整个地方带着一种无法用言语表达的轻快感，让你很难相信自己就处在上海这个大都市周边。身边是众多鸟类，池塘，荷花和长满睡莲的湖畔，走在木头小径与小桥上，可以细细品味东滩多样的气韵与风景。

我不是为看鸟而去，而是为了另一样东西一有机竹子。一个竹子种植园矗立在这大公园的中心地带，所以对我来讲这是一个很好的机会，可以拿一些竹笋来准备我的一道菜。

A different taste of bamboo shoots

不一样的竹笋味道

Western chefs buy bamboo shoots canned in a sticky, smelly juice. Generally, westerners do not use this product because of the smell.

And since we do not use bamboo for cooking as they do in Asia, it's really hard to get it fresh.

I discovered coconut tree shoots in French Polynesia that are similar to bamboo shoots, but the locals use them in salad.

Personally, I prefer to eat bamboo shoots cooked rather than raw. I enjoy them in soups, sauces, and cream. They taste great deep-fried as well.

In the following recipe I highlighted one major product - pork. Chinese love pork. I used plump black pigs from the hills that graze free-range, rather than pigs raised in a factory.

西方厨师通常用竹笋罐头，竹笋带着黏糊糊汁水和不自然的味道。因为这个味道，西方人不爱吃竹笋。如果用亚洲烹饪方式的话，一般又很难找到新鲜竹笋。在法属波利尼西亚发现过新鲜竹笋，他们把它放在沙拉里吃，就像吃椰子树嫩芽一样。就我个人而言，吃竹笋，我爱吃熟的，而不是生的。我喜欢把竹笋放在汤、酱或者奶油里吃，也可以油炸。

接下来的食谱，我想突显猪肉和竹笋的配合。中国人喜欢吃猪肉，但我食谱里用到的猪肉不是工厂饲料猪，而是在山坡上自由放养、圆润健康的黑猪。

Recipe 8
食谱 8

slow-cooked crispy farm-raised pork belly with braised bamboo shoots
慢煮香脆农家五花肉，配焖竹笋

4 Servings

4 人份

Ingredients
配料

500 g ---------- Black pork belly 黑猪腩

100 g ---------- Rock salt 岩盐

Seasoning
调料

2 pieces ---------- Bay leaves 月桂叶

1 pieces ---------- Cinnamon sticks 肉桂条

2 pieces ---------- Star anis 八角

10 pieces ---------- Whole black pepper 整胡椒粒

200 ml ---------- Pork stock 猪肉汤

Bamboo shoots
竹笋

500 g ---------- Bamboo shoots 竹笋

3 g ---------- Sichuan peppercorn 四川胡椒粒

5 g ---------- Sugar 糖

5 ml ---------- Dark soy sauce 老抽

100 ml ---------- Shaoxing cooking wine 绍兴料酒

200 ml ---------- Vegetable stock 蔬菜汤

Chopped green onion 葱碎

Directions
作法

1. For the pork belly:

a. Brush the pork belly meat with the rock salt for 6 hours.

b. Rinse it and blanched the meat in hot water for 10 minutes to remove all impurities.

c. Sear the skin on a pan with the baking paper between the pan and the skin to protect the meat from burning, till the meat is in a golden color.

d. Put the meat in a vacuum bag or a double freezer bag.

e. Add the seasonings and the stock. Seal the bag and put it in the oven at 75 to dry for 12 hours.

f. After cooking, put the meat in the fridge and press it to be flat. Keep it in the fridge for 2 days.

g. Slice a thick piece of the pork and pan sear it on a baking paper to get a very crispy skin.

h. Add some stock if necessary.

i. Take the cooking sauce out and reduce the juice to make a demi-glace sauce.

五花肉：a. 用岩盐刷五花肉刷 6 小时。

b. 冲洗后放入热水灼 10 分钟，去除所有的杂质。

c. 把肉皮垫着烘烤纸一起烤，避免皮和锅直接接触而烤焦，烤至金黄色。

d. 把肉放入真空袋里，或者没有真空袋就放入一个 双层冷冻袋里。

e. 放入调味料和汤汁，密封后放入 75 摄氏度的炉子里 12 小时。

f. 煮好后，把肉放入冰箱里，按平它，放置两天后可用。

g. 把猪肉切成厚片，隔着烘烤纸放入锅中烤至皮脆。

h. 如果需要的话，加入汤汁。

i. 取走多余的汁使其半油渍。

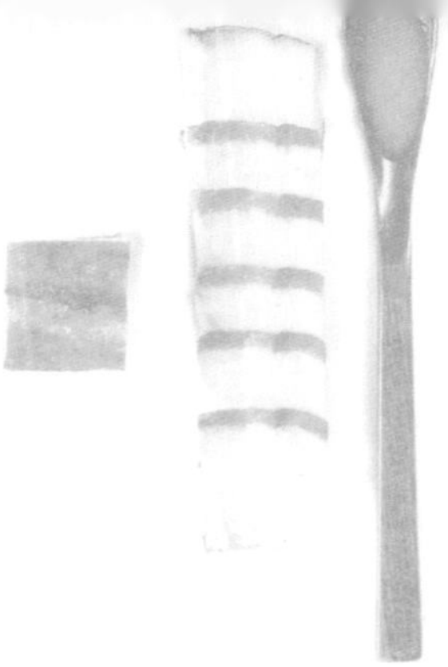

2. For the bamboo shoots:

a. Cut the bamboo lengthwise; cut off the dried bottom.

b. Put them in the pot with the vegetable stock and cook them for 10 minutes.

c. Then cut them into 3 cm cubes.

d. Heat the oil and deep fry the bamboo shoots for 5 minutes until you get a light golden brown color.

e. Add the pepper, cover and cook for 10 more minutes. Remove the pepper.

f. Return the bamboo in a wok, add sugar, dark soy sauce, cooking wine and vegetable stock. Cover and braise in low heat for 20 minutes.

g. Uncover and reduce the sauce by half.

竹笋：a. 把竹子纵向切开，切掉下面干的部分。

b. 和蔬菜汤一起放入锅中，煮 10 分钟。

c. 把其切成边长 3 厘米的小块。

d. 把油加热，把竹笋炸 5 分钟，直至变成淡淡的金褐色。

e. 放入胡椒，盖住并煮 10 多分钟。然后移除胡椒。

f. 把竹子放回锅中，放入糖，老抽，绍兴料酒和蔬菜汤，低温煮烧 20 分钟。

g. 当竹子露出汁面后，把汁酱减半。

3. Set up:

Cut the pork in cubes of 3 by 3 cm; set up the cooked bamboo shoots on side.

摆盘：把猪肉切成 3×3 厘米的立方体，把煮好的竹笋放在一旁。

Your notes

Great recipes are not created, but perfected.
好的食谱来自一次又一次的修改完善。

Note down the changes you make on this recipe to create your very own version of it.
记录下你对这个食谱做的修改，探寻属于你自己的味道。

Chef's tips:
厨师贴士

The choice of the pork is important because you must get a pork belly with more meat than fat to get a meat that is juicy instead of having just a piece of fat. During the slow cooking process the fat will melt and moist the meat, that's why it's important to choose a meaty part of pork belly and not a fatty one.

猪肉的选择非常重要，因为猪肉必须多肉少肥，是多汁的肉而不是一块肥肉。在慢煮的过程中，肥肉会融化，所以选择一块精肉多肥肉少的五花肉很重要。

9

故事九

Yingdong Ecological Village

瀛东生态村

I visited the Yingdong Ecological Village after the Dongtan Wetlands. I felt as if I were in Holland, where people focus on the future and what kind of heritage they will pass down to future generations. These sensibilities are why they develop their industry and economy in such an eco-friendly way, with less pollution and more clean energy.

We arrived there on a Friday afternoon. No one was around. The village looked dead: two small organic shops, a cultural center...nothing special at first glance, except one thing - this village was ecological. I realized that 2007 was too early for the Shanghainese to create an ecological village. They were not yet ready to go ecological.

Wind generators and solar panels were everywhere. With its recycling water system, Yingdong was supposed to be more alive than any other places in Shanghai, yet seemed to be a ghost town.

走过东滩湿地，我去了瀛东生态村。这个村落让人有置身荷兰的感觉，因为跟荷兰一样，这个村子的建设体现了人们关注未来的想法，关注他们留给子孙后代的将是怎样的一个环境。正是基于这样的情感，他们用环保方式发展产业和经济，减少污染，更多采用清洁能源。

我们是一个周五的下午到那里的。没有看到任何人，一点生气也没有。村里有两家小小的有机商店，一个文化中心……第一眼看去没什么特别，除了一件事—这个是一个挂着“生态”名号的村子，肯定得有什么是与众不同的。我心想，对上海人而言，2007 年就创立生态村有点太早，他们还没有准备好迎接与生态和谐并存的生活方式。

村里风力发电机与太阳能电池板随处可见，又有先进水循环系统，瀛东村本该是个脱俗的清新之地，现在却似乎成了一个没有什么活力的空城。

The nation's hope of going ecological...

和谐生态的一场梦

I went straight to the shops to discover what's in a Chinese organic shop. I hit pay dirt! Sold in the shop were: Bai jiu, pickles, grains, vegetables and fruits. So I grabbed a few things and created some recipes centered on these unique items.

This Yingdong ecological village on Chongming Island carries the hope of a once heavily polluted city to close to the great nature again. I would say Chongming Island can be Shanghai's storehouse; everything can be produced and grown from there. After the trip I'm convinced that Shanghainese don't really need to import anything from outside.

That's why in my recipe I used one product I did not find in downtown Shanghai - organic wheat. Everybody uses wheat for bread, dumplings and numerous other delicacies. But in this recipe I used the wheat in different ways, creating a de-light dish made in four simple steps.

我直接去了商店，想看看能在一家中国生态商店里找到些什么宝贝。收获非常不错，他们出售白酒、腌菜、谷物、蔬菜和水果。我在店里随便就能找到不错的食材。用这些食材作为主要材料，我设计了几道菜。

崇明岛上的这个瀛东村所追求的生态和谐和所进行的种种尝试让人感动，每个举动都饱含了上海这个曾经被严重污染的大都市想要重新走近自然的梦想。从另一个面来看，我认为崇明岛完全可以充当上海的粮仓。我甚至觉得，上海根本不需要向上海以外的地方进口任何东西，依靠崇明岛的供给似乎很符合环保低碳的理念。

这就是为什么我在这个故事的食谱中使用了一个我在上海市区找不到的食材，真正的有机小麦。通常小麦会被用来做面包、饺子以及许多其他美味佳肴。但在这个菜谱里，我想尝试用不同的方式去处理小麦这个可塑性极高的食材。简单的四个步骤就可以做一道健康的轻食。

Recipe 9
食谱 9

variations of organic chongming wheat
崇明有机小麦新菜式

6 Servings

6 人份

The Soup
汤

- 700 g ------------ Chopped Toasted Wheat Seeds 烤麦籽碎
- 120 g ------------ Water 水
- 2 sheets ------------ Gelatin 明胶
- little ------------ Truffle oil 松露油
- little ------------ Black truffle 黑松露

Salad
沙拉

- 30 g ------------ Wheat sprouts 麦芽
- 20 g ------------ Wheat bulgur 麦碎
- 10 g ------------ Wheat 小麦
- 10 g ------------ Chopped Shallot 葱头碎
- 20 g ------------ Baby leaves 嫩叶

Dressing
汁酱

- a few drops ------------ Shanxi vinegar 山西醋
- little ------------ Sugar 糖

Directions
作法

1. The Soup:

a. Put the wheat seeds in the water and let them sit for 12 hours.

b. Blend them together to get a smooth texture. Add salt.

c. Warm the soup, add the soft gelatin.

d. Fill a sip with the soup and add the truffle oil.

汤：a. 提前一天把麦切好，加入水，放置 12 小时。

b. 第二天把其搅拌至柔滑的混合物，加入盐。

c. 加热汤，加入明胶片，使其溶化。

d. 倒入一个小容器，添加松露油。

2. The Sala:

a. Germ the wheat seeds for sprouts 3 days ahead.

b. Soak the wheat seed in water.

c. Prepare the dressing by blending all the dressing ingredients together.

沙拉：a. 提前 3 天使胚芽萌发。

b. 把麦籽泡在水里。

c. 准备好汁酱并混合在一起。

Your notes

Great recipes are not created, but perfected.
好的食谱来自一次又一次的修改完善。

Note down the changes you make on this recipe to create your very own version of it.
记录下你对这个食谱做的修改，探寻属于你自己的味道。

Chef's tips:
厨师贴士

You can use other grains to make a similar recipe. To make an Asian or Mexican style dish, you can add some other beans you can find locally. Adding green lentils would add a stronger French flavor to it.

你可以使用其他谷物来制作相类似的食谱，还可以通过加入你在本地能找到的其他豆类来制作亚洲和墨西哥风味的食谱，或者使用绿扁豆来制作法国风味的食谱。

10

故事十

The Chen Jia Zhen Village Market

陈家镇集市

We arrived at the traditional Chinese market at sunset. Warm light caressed the vendor stalls. Some fishermen were selling their fresh catch of the afternoon - live wild eels, crayfish, and river shrimp as well as vegetables and poultry. On a side street I saw two ladies cutting the heads off of Zi Yu, a species of fish from Changjiang river.

Small red fish were drying under the sun. The ladies removed the heads to avoid their bitter flavor. The heads were fed to the pigs; nothing goes to waste in China. This fish had white meat and pink skin, but what made it so special? It's special because you cannot easily find this Artisan style of dried fish in Shanghai. Also, the fish has a distinctive flavor, because river-fish do not taste overly fishy.

With this unique fish I decided to make one of my signature dishes - the French fusion bouillabaisse. This is a light fish broth made in the south of France using rockfish near the coast of the Mediterranean sea. But for my Chinese friends I fused this French soup with the traditional dumpling. Both salt water and fresh water fish are acceptable in this dish.

我们在一天日落的是时候抵达这个传统的中国集市。小摊上洒满金色阳光，渔民们正在出售他们下午刚捕捞的水产一鲜活的野生鳗鱼、小龙虾以及河虾，还有新鲜蔬菜和家禽。一条小路上，我还见到两个女士在切鲻鱼鱼头。鲻鱼是产自长江的一种鱼。小小红鱼在太阳底下晒干。女士们斩掉鱼头，这样鱼干就不会带苦味，而且鱼头还可以用来喂猪。在中国，什么都不浪费。

这种鱼的肉是白色，皮肤是粉色。是什么令它如此特别？因为这种把鱼晒干的方式在上海城区很少见，而且河鱼吃起来腥味也少一点。

用这种独特的鱼，我决定做一道我的招牌菜一交融法式鱼肉汤。这是法国南部的一种清淡鱼汤，用地中海海岸附近的岩鱼做成。为了我的中国朋友，我用传统的饺子来交融这道法式汤品。这道菜用海鱼或淡水鱼都可以。

french fusion bouillabaisse

法式河鱼浓汤

6 Servings

6 人份

Ingredients
配料

1 kg	"Chongming river fish" bones[1]	崇明河鱼骨[1]
200 g	Shallots	葱头
200 g	Carrots	胡萝卜
200 g	Celery	西芹
75 g	Garlic	大蒜
250 g	Fresh tomatoes	鲜番茄
50 g	Tomato paste	番茄酱
1 g	Saffron	红花
75 ml	Olive oil	橄榄油
20 ml	White wine	白葡萄酒
75 g	Egg white	蛋白
15 sheets	Sheets gelatin per litter	明胶片每升

Garnish
装饰

150 g	Celery leaves	西芹叶
30 g	Micro greens	芽菜
30 g	Chive sticks 2 cm	2 厘米韭菜段
350 g	Big tomatos	大号番茄
350 g	Green zucchini	青节瓜

Giant DIM SUM Ravioli
大点心 意式水饺

110 g	River shrimps	河虾
50 g	Soy sauce	酱油
100 ml	Fish stock	鱼汤
10 ml	Lemon juice	柠檬汁
25 ml	Olive oil	橄榄油

Garlic cream
蒜味奶油

125 g	Garlic	大蒜
250 g	Cream cheese	奶油芝士
	Salt/pepper to taste	盐 / 胡椒适量

Saffron cream
红花奶油

1 g	Saffron	红花
250 g	Cream cheese	奶油芝士
	Salt/pepper to taste	盐 / 胡椒适量

Shrimp cream
虾味奶油

200 g	Cooked shrimps of any kind	任何品种的熟虾
10 ml	Olive oil	橄榄油
75 ml	Heavy cream	重奶油
150 g	Lemon	柠檬

Rouille sauce
大蒜蛋黄酱

2	Egg yolk	蛋黄
100 ml	Olive oil	橄榄油
10 g	Garlic	大蒜
1 g	Saffron	藏红花

1. can be replaced with sardine bones. 可用沙丁鱼骨代替

Directions
作法

1. Jelly:

a. Wash the fish bones with cold water; sauté them with the olive oil until you get a light brown color.

b. Sauté separately the carrots, the shallots, the celery and the chopped garlic in big brunoise(cubes 1 mm by 1 mm side).

c. Add all the vegetables to the fish bones pot. Add the diced tomatoes, tomato paste and the saffron, cook for 3 minutes.

d. Pour the wine and add some water at the garnish level to be simmered for 45 minutes. Strain and remove the fat then clarify by pouring the egg white on top of the broth and leave for 2 hours to let the eggs go down. Then pour the broth into a linen to filter it.

e. Soften the gelatin sheets in cold water and add them to the cleared broth.

f. Pour the broth on the soup plate and keep them in the fridge.

鱼骨冻：a. 先用冷水清洗鱼骨，用橄榄油炒鱼骨着色。

b. 胡萝卜 / 葱头 / 西芹和切丁（1 毫米 ×1 毫米）的大蒜分别炒好。

c. 然后放入所有的蔬菜到鱼骨中，放入番茄丁，番茄酱和红花，煮 3 分钟。

d. 倒入白酒，加入一些水至装饰线，焖 45 分钟。沥干并去除脂肪，用蛋清使液体澄清。你需要把蛋白倒到浓汤上，放置 2 小时，让蛋慢慢沉到底部。然后用亚麻布把浓汤过滤。

e. 在冷水中软化明胶片，加入清汤。

f. 把汤倒在汤盘上，放入冰箱保存。

2. Ravioli:

Clean the shrimps. Devein them with a bamboo stick; blanch in a court bouillon (made with carrot, bay leaves, black pepper corn, salt, onion with cloves) or salty water. Refrigerate to let them chill.

意式饺子：把虾仁清洗干净，用竹签去除背部的血管，在清汤（胡萝卜，月桂叶，黑胡椒粒，盐，洋葱瓣）中或盐水中白灼。放入冰箱降温。

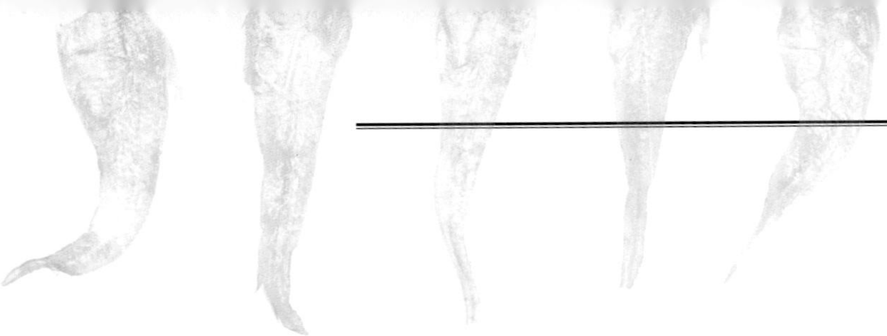

3. Garlic cream:

Blanch the garlic in boiling water 2 times before cooking them slowly in the cream until they are soft. Reduce half of the cream; blend the garlic and cream. Add salt/pepper then strain the mix with the mesh and keep it cold.

蒜味奶油：把大蒜放入沸水中白灼 2 次，然后在奶油中慢煮直至变软。奶油浓缩至一半后搅拌并加入盐 / 胡椒，然后用滤网过滤，保持冷冻。

4. Saffron cream:

Reduce the cream to half by heat; add the saffron, salt/pepper. Strain with the mesh and keep it cold.

红花奶油：把奶油浓缩至一半，放入藏红花，盐 / 胡椒，用滤网过滤，保持冷冻。

5. Shrimp cream:

Strain the cooked shrimps with a mesh; add the olive oil, the cream and lemon juice. Add salt /pepper.

虾味奶油：用滤网把熟虾过滤，加入橄榄油，奶油和柠檬汁，用盐 / 胡椒调味。

6. Garnish:

Make some mini balls with a mini scoop use the special spoon of 0.5 cm diameter. Add the olive oil/salt/pepper. Set up the jelly between the cream drops.

装饰：用 1 个直径 0.5 厘米的小勺制成迷你圆球，加入橄榄油 / 盐 / 胡椒。然后把鱼骨冻放在奶油中间。

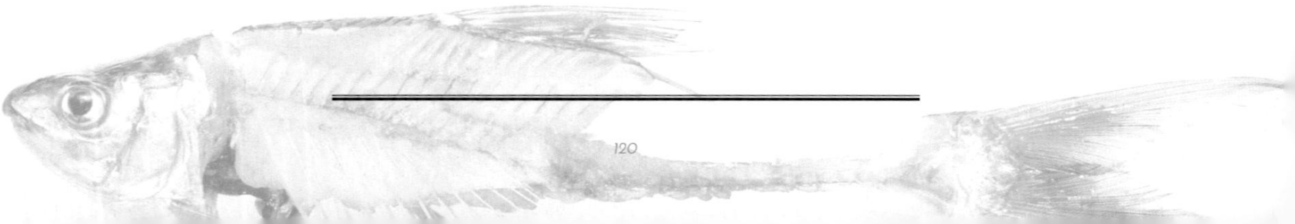

Your notes

Great recipes are not created, but perfected.
好的食谱来自一次又一次的修改完善。

Note down the changes you make on this recipe to create your very own version of it.
记录下你对这个食谱做的修改，探寻属于你自己的味道。

Chef's tips:
厨师贴士

For the fish bones used in this dish, you can choose any white meat sea fish bones. If you cannot find the fresh ones, frozen ones would do as well, but you have to double the quantity of bones because its taste will not be as strong.

做这个菜，你可以选择任意一种白肉海鱼鱼骨。如果你不能够找到新鲜的，冷冻的也可以。但必须用双倍的鱼骨来增强口感，不然味道会不够。

11

故事十一

The Organic Rice Farm

有机水稻农场

Rice is still the principal staple for Chinese people, but it's not easy to produce enough to meet the high demand from the large Chinese population; so for several years Chongming has grown its own rice on the island with 2,000 tons of organic rice annually. Thanks to that, farmers have a better life - increasing profits by fifty percent and growing "pure organic" rice crops, which require no pesticides or chemical fertilizers, which would be too costly for the farms.

The rice fields are near the village, and most of time the women take care of the difficult task of growing and harvesting it. In China - as well as in most Asian countries - women seem to be responsible for the hard labor.

大米仍是中国人的主食。要生产大量高质量大米来满足十几亿中国人的粮食需求并不容易。近几年，崇明岛发展水稻种植业，年产有机大米达到2000 吨。这样的种植业可以帮助农民过上更好的生活，使他们的收入增加百分之五十以上。种植“纯有机”水稻要求不施农药化肥，使得成本大大增加，有一定的困难。

稻田躲在村庄附近。我发现在中国，大多数时候，都是女人承担水稻生长收割的艰巨任务。在中国和许多亚洲国家，似乎女人也要负责艰苦的劳作。

The organic trend

有机大米的风潮

The same thing happened when I was in Thailand - the farmers went to organic products because they could improve their lifestyle and their working condition at the same time. More and more Western chefs have been using rice over the last 10 years with the increased popularity of Asian food. But the newest trend now is to eat quinoa, wheat, whole rice and other healthy grains.
So I decided to take some of this organic rice and make--not a typical western sautéed rice - but a recipe that is based on classic Chinese rice dish.

我在泰国工作时也留意到了当地人对有机大米种植的追求。农民生产有机农产品，借此他们既可以更好地改善生活，又可以提升生活和工作环境。在过去的十多年，因为亚洲菜的流行，越来越多西方厨师纷纷开始使用大米。但现在最新趋势是吃藜麦，小麦，全谷物米饭以及其他健康谷物。

所以我决定用一些有机大米做一道基于传统米饭的菜肴，而不是一般的西式炒饭。

Recipe 11
食谱 11

organic chongming island rice coffee rice foam
崇明岛有机米 -- 咖啡大米泡沫

4 Servings

4 人份

Ingredients
配料

100 g	Organic white rice	有机白米
800 g	Water	水
3 g	Hainan ground coffee	海南咖啡粉
100 ml	Milk	牛奶
50 g	Cream	奶油
5 ml	Cherry vinegar	樱桃醋
	Salt/pepper to taste	盐 / 胡椒适量

Garnish
装饰

1 g	Dry chili powder	辣椒粉
3 g	Salt flake	盐花
1 g	xantana powder[1]	黄原胶粉[1]

1. xantana powder for the espuma bottle (xantana can be replaced with 3 gelatin sheets).
用于泡沫瓶的黄原胶粉（黄原胶可以用 3 片明胶片代替）

Directions
作法

1. Cook the rice with the water and the coffee for 20 minutes.

用水和咖啡把米煮 20 分钟。

2. Blend and strain the water. Keep 200 g of the water.

搅拌并把水过滤掉，留下 200 克的水。

3. Cool down the rice.

冷却米饭。

4. Add the milk, the cream and vinegar and try the taste.

加入牛奶，奶油和醋，调味。

5. Take the rice and spread it on a silicon sheet to make it as thin as possible.

取用剩的米铺在硅胶片上，需要铺足够薄。

6. Sprinkle the chili powder (I use the French one the Espelette Chili, which tastes better than the local one) and the salt; dry in the oven at 65 until the rice is dry.

撒上辣椒粉和盐（我用的是法国的艾斯佩莱特辣椒，比本地的更加美味），在 65℃的炉子里把米烘干。

7. Put the xantana in the espuma bottle; shake well. Keep warm.

把黄原胶放入泡沫瓶中，摇匀，保持温热。

8. Crush the dry rice to be used like rice crackers.

把烘干后的米弄碎，弄成米饼的样子。

Your notes

Great recipes are not created, but perfected.
好的食谱来自一次又一次的修改完善。

Note down the changes you make on this recipe to create your very own version of it.
记录下你对这个食谱做的修改，探寻属于你自己的味道。

Chef's tips:
厨师贴士

You can use any type of rice in this recipe because this recipe focuses more on the amount of starch in the rice. All you need to do is to choose clean rice because you should not wash the rice so as to keep the starch.

这个配方用什么品种的米都可以，因为这里重点的米的淀粉含量。选米的时候选干净的米，因为这个配方要求不能洗米以免影响米的淀粉量。

Part II Downtown Shanghai

第二部分 上海市内

Like most foreigners arriving in a new city, in an unknown country, one needs to find his culinary roots. So I decided to go in an Italian restaurant, the only western restaurant I could find near where I was living. It was not easy finding that place. We had to go through another shop to reach the lift. We arrived on the wrong floor and saw a group of half-dressed men playing cards.

We eventually found the so called "Italian" restaurant. It was the first time I had fresh fruit with lettuce and Thousand Island dressing, experiencing quite a Western and Asian cultural food shock.

But I am not so surprised now when I consider Chinese food in Paris, where only the name is Chinese. The food, however, is a far cry from the truly delicious Chinese cuisine.

After this unusual culinary experience, we tried to hail a cab, but, in the rain, it is really challenging in any big city. When we finally

像大多数来到一个新城市的外国人一样，在一个陌生国度里，人们需要找到自己食味之根。因此，我决定前往一家意大利餐厅，这是我在靠近我住的地方所能找到的唯一一家西方餐厅。找到它一点也不容易。我们不得不穿过另一家店去坐电梯，还坐错楼层发现一群正在光着上身打牌的男子。

等到最终找到，虽然标注着是“意大利餐厅”，但菜式却是有名无实，这是我第一次吃到新鲜水果拌生菜和千岛沙拉酱。这是我感受到的第一个西方和亚洲的食物文化冲击。

但如今想起巴黎的“中餐”时，我就没那么惊讶了。巴黎的中国菜，也只是名字叫中国，与正宗中国美食相距甚远。

经历这不同寻常的饮食体验后，我们试着拦个出租车，但下雨天在任何大城市打车都称得上是个挑战。好不容易等来一辆出租车，不知从哪里冒出一名男子，和我们一块儿往里钻。那次打车经历既是第一次也是最后一次。作为一个专

上海“新世界”
我在上海市区的第一次美食之旅

“New World” Sha

My first culinary experience in downtown Shanghai

got a taxi, another man came from nowhere and jumped inside with us. This was the first and last time that this happened. To be a professional taxi catcher, you must have careful timing and little shame. Now I do not even hesitate to share a ride with strangers, sometimes hiding in the bushes to jump out to try to a cab in the middle of the street.

Nanjing road is like the Champs Elysee for the French: huge, crowded (at least one million Chinese citizens cross this street per day) and where food and fashion are mixed together. The moon cake shop in front of the Sofitel Hyland is packed every day, and people queue in front of the Häagen Dazs store, the reason being its popularity.

It was quite a challenge for a 32-year-old chef to handle such a big hotel in an unknown city. But I was ready for the task.

业的打车高手，你必须瞅准时机，厚起脸皮。现在，我甚至毫不犹豫就会和一个陌生人在出租车上共享一程。为了打车，我甚至还试过躲在路旁的树丛里等着空车出现就跳出来截住。

南京路就像法国的香榭丽舍大道：宽大、拥挤，美食与时尚缤纷融合。每天至少有一百万中国人穿过这条街。索菲特海仑宾馆前的月饼店每天人潮汹涌，旁边的哈根达斯门店也很受欢迎，人们常常在门口排起长队。

对于 32 岁的我，在一个全然陌生的城市运营这么大一家酒店的厨房事务，的确是个挑战。但我已准备好了。

12

故事十二

The Beach and the Baijiu

海滩和白酒

Having lived in Shanghai for two years, I never knew it can be the "Small St Tropez "(St Tropez is a well-known seaside resort in southeastern France).

Shanghai has several beach or huge pool areas you can enjoy in summer time. A friend and I decided to discover the beach area in the South of Shanghai Jinshan which is about 1 hour's drive from downtown. Arriving there, I felt like I was back to a beach resort in France with the same balloons, candy shots and the familiar smell of sunscreen.

There is a dam dividing the polluted water from the industrial area and the beach area. You can tell by the clear water of the sea which resembles that of the Bora Bora lagoon, that the dam is working magic.

A lot of Shanghainese love to go there with their family. Yet, I was surprised to bump into a guy who openly told me that he was there to have some fun with his "close personal friend". There are many things you can do by the beach, such as enjoying the music festival, picking up random seafood on the sand, trying the food stand specialties or simply sunbathing. After a quick stop by the beach, we decided to go visit a Baijiu liquor factory. I was there for a music festival. It was quite unusual for a foreigner to see Chinese people having fun with rock and heavy metal music by the beach, drinking beer and playing games.

在上海住了两年，我从不知道原来它还有"小圣特罗佩斯"(圣特罗佩斯是法国东南著名滨海旅游胜地)的一面。

上海有好几个海滩或大水池区域供人消磨夏日时光。南部金山的海滩，离市区大约一小时的车程，我和一个朋友去探索了一番。到那儿，我感觉自己仿佛回到了法国海滩度假村，那里同样的气球、甜饮和熟悉的防晒霜味道。

这儿有个水坝，把工业区污水与海滩隔开。望着眼前清澈如波拉波拉岛（Bora Bora 是太平洋东南部岛屿）的海水，你就知道这个水坝是有多么地神奇。

许多上海人喜欢和家人去那里放松。有一次，我还碰到个让我大跌眼镜的家伙，他堂而皇之地跟我讲，他是和"亲密友人"来这儿玩。海滩上有很多事可做，你可以享受音乐节，在沙滩捡捡海鲜，尝尝小摊上的特色美味，或者就简单晒晒太阳。在海滩上流连了一会儿，我们就决定去一个白酒厂参观。我是为了音乐节才去海滩的。看中国人在海边玩摇滚、重金属音乐，喝啤酒，玩游戏，对我这个外国人来讲，感觉是挺不寻常的。

Baijiu Liquor Factory

白酒厂飘香

Stopping at the Baijiu liquor factory at The Shenxian baijiu brewing factory, the strong smell of baijiu makes up most of my first impression of the place. Later I learned that is the charm and special touch of baijiu. Baijiu has been one of the most popular liquor drinks for family dinners and important events in China. It is like the Bordeaux wine to the French. There is no good meal without a fine bottle of wine.

Local Chinese think this liquor can also give people a walking-on-clouds experience, making them spiritually free from the real world's troubles for a while. The history of the town's Shenxian liquor dates back to Qing Dynasty (1644-1911). A farmer surnamed Cai opened a shop in the town center, brewing baijiu in an old-fashioned way with a simple steaming wok and using grains such as sorghum and wheat. The ancient technique stretched across generations, as ideas were passed on and embellished. The drink earned its popularity in the town and even spread to the city. I visited this factory and its baijiu museum to learn about the traditional brewing skills. The museum highlights some interesting facts about liquor, illustrates the culture and history of baijiu, along with some folk tales.

Like for all the liquors in any country, there are different grades of baijiu. It is complex like the Cognac from France. The classification is based on the fragrance, the year and the flavors.

The technique of brewing is different in different provinces in China depending on the grain they are using. The price can be as cheap as a beer or more expensive than a Chateau Margaux.

进入这家名为“神仙酒厂”的白酒厂，一股强烈的白酒味扑面而来，给我留下了很有趣的第一印象。稍后，我得知这浓烈的味道就是白酒的独特与魅力之所在。

在中国，白酒是家庭聚餐与重大宴席上最流行的酒精饮品。就像波尔多葡萄酒之于法国，这里，一个像样的宴席，上好的白酒不可或缺。当地中国人觉得白酒能给人一种遨游云端的美妙体验，让人在精神上短暂地远离尘世烦扰。这个镇上神仙酒的历史可上溯到清代（1644–1911）。一个姓蔡的农民在小镇中央开家店，以一个简单的汽蒸锅为工具，高粱和小麦等谷物做材料，用传统方式酿造白酒。古代工艺代代相传，如同被传承与发扬的思想一样。这种酒在小镇上流行起来，然后在整个城市流行起来。为了解传统的酿造技艺，我参观了这家工厂和它的白酒博物馆。博物馆凸显了关于白酒的一些趣闻，介绍了白酒的文化和历史，以及一些民间故事。

就像任何国家的各种酒一样，白酒也分不同的等级，复杂程度一如法国干邑的等级划分。它的划分标准则基于香气、年份以及口味。不同省份有不同的白酒酿造技术，这取决于所用的谷物。白酒的价格有的像啤酒一般便宜，有的比玛歌酒庄珍酿更昂贵。

Recipe 12
食谱 12

lao bai jiu 21 days foie gras, drunken river shrimps
老白酒 21 天肥肝，配醉河虾

Preparation time 21 days
准备时间 21 天

Ingredients
配料

60 g ---------- Rougie Foie gras 露杰鸭肝

40 ml ---------- Lao Bai Jiu 老白酒

15 g ---------- Salt 盐

3 g ---------- White pepper 白胡椒

2 g ---------- Sugar 糖

3 Kg ---------- Duck fat 鸭肥

12 ---------- Steamed buns 蒸馒头

Garnish
装饰

15 g ---------- Sea salt flower 海盐花

7 g ---------- Black peppercorn 黑胡椒粒

1 Kg ---------- Fig and cinnamon country bread toasted 无花果和肉桂乡村面包土司

Cinnamon stick 肉桂条

Drunken River shrimps
醉河虾

3 Kg ---------- Duck fat 鸭肥

300 g ---------- River shrimps 河虾

200 ml ---------- Lao Bai Jiu 老白酒

Directions
作法

1. Lao Bai Jiu 21 days foie gra:

a. Pour on the foie gras some Bai jiu and add the seasoning. Wrap it with the plastic film for 1 night.

b. Put the foie gras in room temperature the next day.

c. Warm the duck fat in an oven (put a thermometer next to the fat) to 80°C in an oven heated up to 110°C.

d. Turn the oven temperature down to 80°C.

e. Put the foie gras in the fat for 25 minutes. (The temperature inside the liver must be 54°C.

f. Take it out and drain it for 2 hours, then wrap it with plastic film to give it an oval sausage shape of 6 cm diameter.

g. Put the foie gras in a deep bucket and pour in the cold duck fat, let it sit for 20 days.

老白酒 21 天肥肝：a. 在肥肝上撒上少许白酒和调味料，用保鲜膜包裹好放置 1 晚。

b. 第二天把肥肝放置在室温下。

c. 把鸭肥放入 110 摄氏度的炉中加温至 80 摄氏度（在鸭肥旁放入温度计观察温度）。

d. 然后把温度降至 80 摄氏度。

e. 把肥肝放入鸭肥中 25 分钟（肥肝内温度必须为 54 摄氏度）。

f. 取出风干 2 小时，然后包裹成直径为 6 厘米的香肠状椭圆形。

g. 把肥肝放入深桶中，倒入冷鸭肥，放置 20 天。

2. Shrimps:

a. Peel and devein the shrimps; Warm them up with a little baijiu to remove the strong smell while keeping the original taste of the shrimps.

b. Just blanch them quickly for about 10 seconds.

虾仁：a. 把虾仁去皮并去血管，用白酒稍微加热以去除强烈的味道，并保持虾仁的口味。

b. 然后快速白灼 10 秒钟。

3. Set up:

a. Slice the foie gras in thick slices of 2 cm; you can put some cracked black peppers on the side and some extra salt as well if the seasoning is not enough for you.

b. Serve a side of plain steam bun.

摆盘: a. 把肥肝切成厚度 2 厘米的片，如果调味料不够，可放些黑胡椒碎和盐在边上。

b. 配着馒头上菜。

Your notes

Great recipes are not created, but perfected.
好的食谱来自一次又一次的修改完善。

Note down the changes you make on this recipe to create your very own version of it.
记录下你对这个食谱做的修改，探寻属于你自己的味道。

Chef's tips:
厨师贴士

I choose the Rougie foie gras for its consistency and the high quality of their overall products. They guarantee over 80 days for the ducks and geese to be raised in free range farm.

我选用露杰肥肝是因为这个品牌的肥肝口感浓郁，整体产品都能保持高质量。露杰保证他们的鸭和鹅在牧场里放养超过 80 天，品质独一无二。

13

故事十三

A Turning Point in My Life

我生命中的转折点

It may seem impossible but I lost 70 pounds in 6 months and keep it off for good.

Thanks to my wife, I met someone in April 2011 who has changed my life: a nutritionist and acupuncture therapist, Viviane. This lady has changed my way of eating with her profound knowledge in Chinese medicine. It's not until the moment I met her that I realized the importance of a balanced diet, which later has helped improve the menus I design. Many westerners fly cross lands and seas to seek advice from Viviane.

So how did she change my life? She helped me understand that:

"Eating is not an obligation but a need"

听起来可能有点不可思议，但是我在6个月内瘦了70磅（约31.7公斤），而且现在一直保持减肥后的体重。

感谢我的妻子，她让我在2011年4月认识了营养师、针灸医生Viviane。正是这位女士改变了我的饮食习惯，也改变了我的人生。她让我意识到维持一日三餐饮食平衡的重要性。有很多西方人不远万里来到中国向她请教，让她帮忙解决不同的健康问题。

那么她是如何改变我生活的呢？很简单，她让我懂得：

"吃不是一项义务，而是一种需要"

上海建工
OXBOW

Traditional Chinese Medicine

For the Chinese, a balanced diet is essential to health, especially for the Cantonese, whereas the westerners find the concept of Ying and Yang bewildering.

In traditional Chinese medicine, disease is caused by the imbalance in the organ system or chi, the vital energy which circulates in channels called meridians , and the goal of any remedy or treatment is to help obtain the innate harmony. Disease can be caused by internal factors like emotions, or external factors such as the environment and weather, or others such as injuries, trauma, diet, and germs.

However, infection is primarily not seen as a problem with germs and viruses, but a weakness in the energy of the body that incurs sickness. Illnesses are treated differently as each body has its own characteristics. Acupuncture relieves or adjusts the flow of chi throughout the organ system, strengthening the body and facilitating self-healing. Acupuncture is one of the most practiced health treatments in China. It involves the use of sharp, thin needles that are inserted in the body at very specific points, which is believed to be able to adjust and alter the body energy flow into healthier patterns.

CHI

Another fundamental concept of Chinese medicine is that of chi, pronounced chee, also spelled qi. Chi is believed to be the invisible but omnipresent life force of the whole universe. In the body, it is the vital energy that creates and animates life. We have inherited chi from nature and parents. After we were born we acquire chi from the air we breathe and from the water and food we take in. Then we form the chi of emotional activities which is affected by the surrounding environment. The level and quality of a person's chi also depends on the state of physical, mental and emotional balance.

中医

对于中国来人，尤其是广东人，食物均衡与身体健康息息相关。然而，这里的阴阳概念却让西方人摸不着头脑。

据中医理论，疾病是由脏腑、气血、经络运行失调所致。任何疾病治疗的目标都是帮助身体恢复内部的调和。疾病可能由内部因素如情绪引起，也可能起于外部因素像环境和天气，还受诸如跌打损伤、饮食和细菌等其他因素影响。

然而，在中医看来，疾病并非源自细菌和病毒，而是体虚的表现。没有两种疾病是相同的，因为每个人的身体所表现出来的症状和平衡都不相同。针灸可以开启或调整脏腑中气的运行，以达到强健体魄使身体自愈的目的。针灸是中医治疗中的主要形式之一。它用尖而细的针刺入身体中特定的穴位，这个过程是经过疏通经络、调和气血，来治疗各种各样的疾病。

气

中医的另一个基本概念是“气”。气是宇宙的基本生命能量。它是无形的，存在于空气、水、食物和阳光中。在人体内，它是创造生命活力的重要力量。出生时，我们带有先天的精气，我们从摄入的食物与吸入的空气中获取后天之气。人体内气的健康水平还取决于身体、精神和情绪的调和状况。气运行于体内的经络之中。

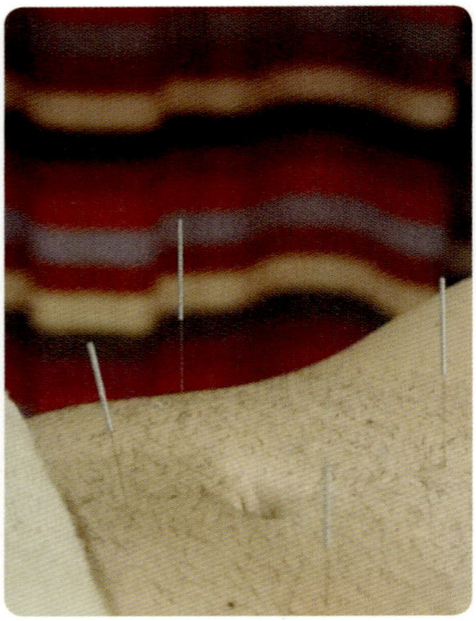

THE FIVE ELEMENTS (WU XING)

Wu Xing is the principal theory of Chinese philosophy which believes that the world is made up of five main elements: wood, fire, earth, metal, and water. These elements are all interconnected. Each element either generates or overcomes another element. For instance, water controls fire and earth generates metal. Each organ is associated with one of the five elements. The Chinese system theory uses elements and organs to describe and treat conditions. The kidney is associated with water while the heart correlates with fire, and these two organs are related the way as water and fire. If the kidney weakens, there might be a corresponding fire problem in the heart. Then the treatment might be acupuncture or herbs to cool the cardiac system and/or boost the energy of kidney system.

五行

中医理论的另一个基础是五行说，认为世界和人体是由金、木、水、火、土五种主要元素构成。这些元素相互关联，每种元素与其他元素相生相克。例如，水克火、土生金。人体的每个脏腑组织都对应一种元素。中医体系运用五行和五脏的对应来阐释和治疗疾病。

例如，肾属水，心属火，肾与心的关系类似于水与火的关系。如果肾虚，则可能是心中火气亢热，所以治疗方法应该是用针灸或中药来降心火抑或是滋补肾元。

THE ORGAN SYSTEM

In the Chinese medicine theory on body system, there are twelve main organs: the lung, stomach, spleen, heart, kidney, liver, urinary bladder, gallbladder, large intestine, small intestine, pericardium, and the "triple warmer". Each organ is characterized by the chi associated and a particular human emotion. As there are twelve organs, there are twelve types of chi that travel through the twelve main channels or meridians. Chinese doctors connect symptoms to corresponding organs. That is, symptoms are caused by yin/yang imbalance in one or more organs, or by an abnormal flow of chi. Each organ has a particular column of symptoms as manifestation.

脏腑组织

在中医体系中，有十二个主要的器官：肺、大肠、胃、脾、心、小肠、膀胱、肾、肝、胆囊、心包和“三焦”，它们代表的是整个躯干内的器官。每个器官都有气与之关联，并与特定情绪相互作用。人体有十二个器官，也有十二种气通过十二条主要经络运行于体内。中医将病症与器官相联系，认为病症是由一个或多个器官内阴阳失衡或者是气从一个器官到另一器官流布不顺所引起的。每个器官都表现出不同的症状。

YIN AND YANG

Yin and Yang are the most fundamental concepts in traditional Chinese philosophy, and also the primary guideline in traditional Chinese medicine as principle for diagnosis and treatment.

The earliest reference to Yin and Yang is in the I Ching (Book of Changes) approximately in 700 BC. In this work, all phenomena are said to be the physical presence of Yin-Yang.

The idea of yin and yang is also applied in food and cooking. Yang foods are believed to increase the body's heat, while Yin foods are believed to decrease it. There is a generalization out there that Yang foods tend to be rich in food energy while Yin foods tend to have higher water content. Therefore the ideal way to eat is having both types of food to keep the body in "balance". A person eating too much Yang food might suffer from acne and bad breath while a person eating too much Yin food might be lethargic or anemic.

阴和阳

阴和阳是传统中医里最基本的一组概念，它也是诊断和治疗疾病的基础。约公元前 700 年，《易经》一书中最早提到阴阳的概念。在这本书中，所有的现象都由阴阳来解释。阴阳的思想也被应用到烹饪领域。人们认为阳性食物可以增加身体的热量，而阴性食物的作用则刚好相反。

阴阳这两个概念还被应用于食物与烹饪之中。阳性食物往往集中了食物中的能量，尤其是来自脂肪的能量，而阴性食物则通常含水量较高。中国人希望同时摄取这两种属性的食物以维持体内的调和。一个人吃了太多阳性食物可能患痤疮和带口臭，而吃了太多阴性食物则可能会萎靡不振或出现贫血。

The Chinese classify food in two main categories: Hot and Cold

中国食物的两大分类：热与冷

Chinese food or nutrition therapy is a modality of traditional Chinese medicine. Central to this belief system is the idea that certain foods have a "hot" or heat-inducing quality while others have a "cold" or chilling effect on the body and its organs and fluids. An imbalance of this "heat" and "cold" is said to increase susceptibility to sickness or to directly cause disease itself. Such an imbalance is not necessarily related to the subjective feeling of being hot (e.g. sweating) or cold (e.g. shivering).

A lot of people have confused or misunderstood some Asian precepts. In brief everything we are doing somehow has collateral effects on our body and naturally our life. For example, our eating habits are a contributing factor in our body balance. My doctor in Shanghai taught me different ways to release the stress at work such as taking the time to eat, taking some breaks when it's necessary. Now I have started a new life in a healthier life style.

食疗是传统中医一种愈疾防病的方法。这一理论认为，某些食物偏“热”，另一些食物偏“寒”，这两种属性都会作用到人体上。冷热失调会增加患病的可能性，也会直接导致疾病。这种失调并不一定与觉热（易出汗）和觉冷（易颤抖）的主观感受相关联。

许多西方人误解了一些亚洲人的信条，以至于最后对中医的理解有很大的偏差。

简言之，我们生活中的一切行为都会对我们的身体和生命产生某种影响。我们的饮食习惯与我们身体的调和密切相关。我在上海的医生教会了我许多在工作中释放压力的方法，比如，吃饭时多花一点时间，在必要时就休息一会儿。现在我已经开始以一种更为健康的生活方式去生活。

The keys for a good diet

最佳减肥法的要点

☒ You can not

· **Eat the premade sauce or even the low fat premade food**
吃预制酱料或号称低脂肪的预制食品

You don't know what is in the premade sauce or food. You need to reduce fats of any types.

你无法知道这些食品里面到底有什么配料。你需要减少摄入任何形式的脂肪。

· **Consume too much sugar, not even artificial sugar**
吃太多糖，人造糖也不可以

Don't even put balsamic vinegar in your seasoning to avoid the use of sugar. You can use a lime juice or red wine vinegar instead.

调味香醋也尽量避免，你可以用柠檬汁或红葡萄酒醋代替。

· **Skip a meal 跳过某一餐不吃**

Always have a green apple with you so you will have something healthy to eat, which could also release your stress.

随身带着一个青苹果，这样你想吃东西时就会有健康的东西可以吃，这样也可以释放你的压力。

· **Have big dinners 吃丰盛的晚餐**

It's better to have a soup and stay away from proteins in your dinner while you are in a diet.

在节食期间，晚餐最好只吃一个汤，并避免摄入蛋白质。

· **Have fruits after 7 p.m.7 点后吃水果**

The acidity of the fruit will disturb your sleep

水果中的酸性会影响你的睡眠。

· **Eat too much at one time 一次吃太多**

Do extreme sport that gives you over 120 pulses per minute)

做极限运动（任何让你脉搏超过 120 次 / 分钟的运动）。

· **Have alcohol too often 经常喝酒**

Having occasional drinks is fine.

偶尔喝酒是可以的，但不可以天天喝。

☑ You can

· **Eat 5 times a day (3 meals and 2 snacks)**
每天进食五次（三次正餐和两次零食）

· **Have a lot of vegetables and fruits 多吃水果蔬菜**

· **Steamed or boiled food is better 吃蒸、煮食物**

· **Adapt your meal according to your actual activity (sport, fitness, relaxation) of your day.**
根据你的活动（运动，健身，娱乐），选择你的饮食

· **Eat when you feel hungry 感觉饿时就进食，别挨饿**

· **Do not eat just because it's time to eat, only when it's necessary.**
不必刻板地遵守吃饭时间，饿的时候才吃。

· **You can enjoy all kinds of food but in a small quantity**
你可以享受各色美食，但要适量

· **As for bread, only those of low glycemic level (e.g. the bread of whole flour, T 60 or T80)**
只吃升糖指数低的面包（例如全麦面包、升糖指数 60 或 80 的面包）

· **Do cardio exercise daily. Do not just run fast.**
每天坚持做有氧运动，不单只是快跑。

· **Drink lots of herbal tea (3 liters per day)**
喝大量的草药茶（每天 3 升）

To achieve your desired goal in a diet, you must stabilize your weight at least 3 years to control the fat cells.

想要达到最佳的减肥效果，你必须在至少三年内保持稳定的体重，以控制脂肪细胞。

These advices I'm giving here about diet are more or less universal. Advices here involves some personal directions on a daily basis.

这些要点差不多适合所有人，它们的得来是基于我的亲身体验，希望可以给大家减肥的饮食计划指一个方向。

A 3 Michelin stars chef who focuses on diet

一位关注节食的三星米其林大厨

This perspective on diet has been consolidated in July 2011 by the 3 Michelin stars chef Regis Marcon in France during a cooking training with his team. He introduced his diet rules to me and I was surprised to learn that bread and pasta are allowed in the diet. "Your diet depends only on your physical activity" he said, "For instance, reduce carbs or sugar when you are not having any sport activity and vice versa. Thanks to this training, I have a deeper understanding of dieting, which later has changed of way I make breads. I now focus more on the use of flour with low glycemic level.

三星米其林大厨 Regis Marcon 及其团队在 2011 年 7 月法国举行的烹饪培训中强调了这一节食方法。他向我介绍这个节食法则的时候，我很惊讶地发现他允许在节食中摄入面包和意大利面。“你的饮食安排要根据你的身体活动来设计”他说，“当你不做体育活动的时候，减少碳水化合物或糖的摄入，反之亦然。”

参加了他的培训后，我提高了自己安排饮食的能力，改变了我制作面包的方法，更多地使用低升糖指数的面粉。

Note: The diet and schedule are based on my personal experience and my understanding of healthy living, but it is, after all, not clinical experiment done by medical professionals. Please consult with your doctor or nutritionist before following my dieting advice.

备注：这个节食安排是根据我对健康饮食的理解和我的节食亲身经历而设计的，但是这毕竟不是专业医学人士做的临床试验，而且每个人的体质不同。请读者在采用我的节食建议前询问专业医生或营养师的意见。

This diet schedule can help you lose weight quickly, about 1.5 Kg per week. Yet this diet won't work properly if you are not determined. I use the acupuncture to release my stress and to balance my body besides following this schedule. Thanks to this diet that has changed my life style, many things in my life have changed in the last 3 years, especially the way I design my menu and create my recipes. Now I follow some dietetic balance I never applied before.

这个节食减肥日程可以帮助你快速减肥，平均可以每周减去 1.5 公斤。但是你必须要有足够的决心去给你的生活做出相应的改变，否则很难收到预期的效果。除了用这个减肥日程外，我还接受针灸来释放压力和调和身体平衡。归功于这种生活方式，在过去的三年中，我的生活也发生了极大的变化。其中最主要的是，我大大地改变了我写菜单，制作食谱的方式。我现在遵循着我从未有过的均衡饮食方式。

21:00

上床睡觉 Time for bed

19:00

晚餐时间 Dinner

蔬菜汤 Vegetable soup

不吃含碳水化合物的食物 Avoid the carbs

沙拉 Salad

蔬菜 Vegetables

水 / 茶 Water/Tea

点心时间 Snack

You can have fruit or a bar of dark chocolate

你可以吃一个水果、一块黑巧克力

15:00

12:00

吃午饭 Lunch

适量摄入一些含蛋白质的食物 Take in some proteins in a reasonable amount

不吃含碳水化合物的食物（如汉堡、比萨、三明治）Avoid the carbs (burger, pizza, sandwich)

沙拉（无酱汁、可以加柠檬汁或醋）Salad (no dressing except for lime juice or vinegar)

蔬菜（蒸或煮）Vegetables (steamed or boiled)

水果 Fruits

水 / 茶 Water/Tea

A perfect day of dieting

一个完美的日常饮食安排

"The organs in our body do not share one rhythm. Different organs follow different schedules. For example, certainly the brain is not doing its best work when we wake up in the morning, so it's important to follow a daily schedule to optimize your diet.

你要明白身体各部分器官有不同的节奏和规律，例如你的脑袋在一天刚醒来时通常不会是最佳状态，所以遵循时间表以合理安排饮食很重要。"

05:00

Wake up 起床

Do some physical exercises (Tai Shi) and relax your body by taking a deep breath
做一些体育锻炼例如太极，深呼吸来放松身体

Take a shower 淋浴

Drink water and tea 喝水和茶

07:00

Breakfast 吃早饭

Fruits, fresh juice, brown toast, cream cheese, tea(No Danish pastry, no butter, no jam, no eggs)
新鲜水果，果汁，烤面包，奶酪，茶（不要吃丹麦式的高热量面包，不要加黄油、果酱，不要吃蛋）

Note: 特别提示
You can wake up at 7 a.m. and have your breakfast in your working place.
你也可以早上七点起床，然后在你工作的地方吃早餐。

0:00

Snack 吃点小吃

Fruit is the best choice; avoid the carbs (bread, biscuits...)
最好吃水果，不吃含碳水化合物的食物（如面包，饼干等）

I am having apples because it's crunchy so I can release my stress when I chew.
我通常吃一个苹果，咬一口，脆脆的口感可以释放我的压力。

The perfect diet food product made in Shanghai

上海制造的健康食品

In Shanghai, I found a small shop of home-made noodle on a street. The Laoban ("Owner" in Chinese) and his wife have been making noodles for 30 years, using a rusty machine that looked like it was from another era. He told me that this old machine worked much better than any modern machines you can find on the market. And I was amazed when he showed me his noodles making awards from contests in Shanghai that can be traced back to 20 years ago. I was fortunate to have the chance to enjoy his noodles.

Noodles are an essential ingredient and staple in Chinese cuisine. The variety of Chinese noodles differs based on the region of production, ingredients, shape or width, and manner of preparation. It is an important part of most regional cuisines within China, as well as in Taiwan, Singapore, and other Southeast Asian nations with large overseas Chinese populations.

Chinese-style noodles have also entered the cuisines of neighboring East Asian countries such as Korea (jajangmyeon) and Japan (ramen), as well as Southeast Asian countries such as Vietnam, the Philippines, Thailand, and Cambodia. Noodles were first recorded in history in the East Han dynasty in the first century A.D.

我在上海停留期间在一条街道上发现了一个小面条厂。工厂老板和他的妻子做了 30 年面条。他们使用的面条制作工具看起来非常老旧，像是另一个时代的产物，但却还能非常出色地运作。老板告诉我，这台旧机器比其他任何你在市场上可以找到的现代化机器都好用。看到这位老板 20 年前在上海面条比赛中获得的奖项很让人感动，他自豪地向我展示他获得的所有奖项。随后我还非常有幸地享用到了他做的面条。

面条作为主食是中国菜重要的组成部分。中国面条种类繁多，根据不同的生产区域、原料、形状或宽度来划分。制作面条的准备工作和做意大利面相类似。在新加坡和其他具有相当多华裔人口的东南亚国家，面条也是其饮食的重要组成部分。中式面条也传入了邻近的东亚国家，如韩国的美食（炸酱面）和日本的拉面，还传到了多个东南亚国家，如越南，菲律宾，泰国，柬埔寨。面条的制作在公元一世纪的东汉朝时期就有记载。

Recipe 13
食谱 13

stretched noodles with pickles
兰州拉面

Ingredients
配料

100 g	Bread flour	红牡丹面粉（高筋）
50 g	Snow vegetable	雪菜
100 g	Vegetable	蔬菜
100 g	Wild bamboo shoots	饭扫光（野竹笋）
1	Egg	鸡蛋
100 g	Beef brisket	牛胸肉
	Mineral water	矿泉水

Directions
作法

1 Mix the flour with the egg to make a paste. Let it sit on the table for 30 minutes.

先将面粉，鸡蛋搅拌成面团，静置 30 分钟。

2 Fry the sliced beef brisket.

将牛胸肉切片炒熟。

3 Press the paste by machine. Stretch it several times. Meanwhile add some mineral water to form the noodle shape.

将面团过机，反复将面团拉长，加入枧水，拉成面条。

4 Put the noodles into the boiling water to cook, then add the beef and snow vegetable before you serve it.

放入热水中煮熟，再加入炒熟的牛肉片和雪菜即可。

14

故事十四

The Traditional VS The Modern

传统与现代的碰撞

When Shanghai was elected to host the World Expo in 2010, the local authorities decided to create a "New Shanghai". They wanted to show the rest of the world that China is a modern super-power, like Beijing did during the Olympic games in 2008. New Shanghai was founded with the hopes of erasing China's negative image - the image of a country lacking freedom and sanitation. Many changes were planned to develop a "Better City Better Life", which was the slogan for this - the biggest worldwide event ever organized.

A Giant Project

- $45,000,000,000 spent on the highways, metro, park, renovations, bridges, airport terminal

- 73,000,000 visitors - 95% from China

- 191 Countries - 2,000,000 volunteers

To mark Shanghai as the leading megalopolis in Asia, many changes were made inside the town: pollution from old factories were tackled, parks and greenery proliferated, purification plants were installed to cleanse wastewater, and timeworn districts were renovated.

But despite all those changes, Shanghai still kept some of its former traditions.

2010 年上海被成功推选为世博会举办城市后，就像 2008 年举办奥运的北京一样，当地政府决定要创造一个"新上海"，向全世界展示中国的现代化国家形象，消除不自由国度、不干净之类的误解。

上海，这个中国最大的城市，第一次举办这样世界级的盛会。为实现"城市，让生活更美好"的主题，上海在许多地方做出改变计划。

一个巨大的项目

−450 亿美元花在高速公路、地铁、公园、桥梁、机场航站楼等 −7300 万参观者，其中 95% 来自国内

−191 个国家 −200 万志愿者

把上海作为亚洲主要的国际大都市呈现给世界，这个城市由内到外发生了翻天覆地的变化：消除旧工厂污染，改善绿色空间，净化工厂废水，老城区改造。

新的改变并没有扼杀过去的味道，上海仍保存着部分过去的传统。

The Wok Brothers Xin Yi Iron Wok Shop

铁锅兄弟，新艺（音）铁锅店

I was gliding on my roller blades near the counterfeit market near Baotong lu when I discovered a distinct local district. Old Shanghainese houses, small shops, a cobbler, an ironsmith in the street, and a small wet market deliver an authentic sample of the Shanghai life. However, this ambiance has begun to disappear with the advancement of modern construction and technology.

I was the only laowai in this area. It is not a touristic place as there is nothing to attract either Chinese or foreign tourists. But for me the cherry on the cake was when I discovered a small wooden shed at the end of the lane where the Cen Brothers hammer out homemade woks.

For a chef to see that in middle of nowhere is really unique when you realize the Cens are the last ones making these handmade woks in downtown Shanghai. They produce one wok a day, depending on the size.

Many Chinese chefs from Shanghai and Guangdong order woks from the brothers because they make the woks according to the chef's individual cooking style.

I also discovered that when you get a new wok you do exactly the same thing as when you get a new iron skillet, you oil it with cooking oil or a piece of lard to make it non-stick.

我穿溜冰鞋在宝通路、假货市场那一带闲逛的时候，发现了一个真正意义上的上海区域，街上是老上海房子，各种小店，当街做鞋、当街焊铁的，小鱼和蔬菜市场……一个原汁原味的上海本地生活样本。现代化建筑和新科技的冲击下，这种老上海氛围正在日渐消失。

我是这个地方唯一的“老外”。这里不是旅游区，没什么可吸引中外游客的地方。但当我在小巷尽头发现一个小木屋，当中有姓岑的一对兄弟在捶打铁锅时，对我而言，感觉就像发现了新大陆，可激动了。这真的很难得，在这样一个偏僻的地方，一个法国厨师遇见了上海中心城区仅剩的手工制铁锅工匠。他们一天做一个铁锅（依铁锅大小而定）。

他们根据厨师的烹饪风格制造铁锅，因而总能拿到不少上海和广东厨师的订单。原来，处理一个新铁锅的方法和处理一个新平底锅的方法一模一样，用食用油或者一块肥猪肉涂抹，使得它没那么容易粘锅。

The Shikumen, YongKang Road
—Meeting with a man full of stories

石库门，永康路
—遇见一个充满故事的人

Shikumen (Chinese: 石库门, "Stone Warehouse Gate") is a traditional Shanghainese architectural style which first appeared in the 1860's that combines Western and Chinese elements.

There were 9,000 shikumen-style buildings in Shanghai, comprising 60 percent of the total houses of the city at the time. Today, however, the proportion is much lower. Shikumens are two to three stories structures resembling Anglo-American terraced townhouses. High brick walls enclosing a narrow front yard distinguish these houses. The name "stone gate" references these strong gateways.

Each residence abuts another and all are arranged in straight side lanes called longtang (Chinese: 弄堂). The entrance to each alley is usually surmounted by a stylistic stone archway. This style of housing was devised when local developers adapted Western-style terrace houses to Chinese conditions.

The wall was added to protect against fighting and looting during the Small Swords Rebellion, but proved useful against burglars and vandals during the social upheavals of the early twentieth century as well. By World War II, more than 80% of the city's population lived in shikumen dwellings. Many of these were hastily built based on slum standards, while some were of sturdy construction and featured modern amenities such as running water and flushing toilets.

During and following World War II, massive population increases in Shanghai led to the

石库门，最早出现在 1860 年代，是一个融合中西方元素的上海传统建筑形式。上海曾有石库门建筑 9000 幢，占住宅总量的 60%，但如今这个比例已大幅降低。石库门为两到三层建筑，与北美阶梯屋、城区住宅类似，突出特点是高大砖墙封闭着一个窄前院。“石库门”这个名字指的就是它坚固的门框。

建筑彼此相连，布置形成的整齐街巷就是“弄堂”。街巷入口有装饰性的石质门楣。这种风格的房子是当地人把西式阶梯屋中国化的结果。围墙的修建是为了在小规模动乱中，保护人们免受战斗劫掠之苦。随后，在动荡的二十世纪初，它也有效防止了窃贼和破坏分子。

二战时，80% 的上海人住在这种民居里。许多建造匆忙，只是依照贫民窟的标准建造。也有一些建构坚固，安装

subdivision of many shikumen houses. Spacious living rooms were often divided into three or four smaller rooms, each lent out to a separate family. These cramped conditions continue to exist in many of the shikumen districts that have survived the recent development since the Reform and Opening-up period.

The size and decoration of the shikumen can usually indicate a family's social rank. Many shikumen have amazing woodcraft on the doors the façade and, of course, the furniture. At that time the trend was to mix traditional Chinese furnishings with a western flair such as a phonograph, camera, radio, or lamp.

Encountering an traditional Chinese family

After 2 years in Shanghai I still had not had the chance to visit a traditional Chinese house. I was walking down the street one day when I noticed a large wooden door at the main entrance of a Shikumen.

After going through a lot of troubles, I finally met the owner of this residence -- a language teacher at a university. While giving a tour of the house, he described the life before the

有自来水和抽水马桶等现代设施。二战期间和二战后，上海人口激增，致使许多石库门建筑被改造和细分以容纳更多的人。

比如，宽敞的客厅分割成了三四间房，每间房出租给一户人家。如此局促的居住条件在许多石库门地区持续存在到改革开放后。

石库门的大小和装饰，反映着一个家庭的社会地位。

许多石库门建筑的门、房屋正面和所有家具上，都有非常精致的木雕。那一时期，社会风潮就是西方时尚（留声机、摄影机、收音机、照相架、电灯）与中国传统交融一体。

遇见传统中国房屋人家

在上海两年，我并没有什么机会去参观一间传统的中国房屋。一天在街上走着，我突然留意到一间有木制大门的石库门房子。

就这样，我有幸见到了这个地方的主人。他是一所大学语言类的老师。他带我参观了整座建筑，向我讲述了这座房子文革前后的故事。他们家曾是中产阶级，所以在上海拥有自己的房子，一家人住一块儿，后来房子要被分出来，一间房就住了一户人家。

主人向我描述每间房，他家人在里面做什么，讲述一些家庭故事，孩子的诞生或后一代的喜事。他与我分享了他的过去和一些有趣的本地传统习惯。

Cultural Revolution, and recounted some changes that were made after. His family was middle-class, so they owned a private house in Shanghai for the family, but later this family house was shared with other families -- one family per room. He described each room, what his family did inside, and some family events such as celebrating weddings and new births. This man shared with me a part of his past and some different traditional rituals.

For instance, early in the morning his mother brought a traditional red wooden excrement and urine bucket to wait for a coach to pick up the bucket. In the street all other families were doing the same ritual. They would chat with each other while waiting for the coach. The red wooden bucket is a Chinese traditional item that was commonly gifted to newlyweds, sometimes with money or goods inside.

His house and all the surrounding area were supposed to be destroyed several years ago by the municipalities before the world expo, but the question was, where would they rehouse all those people? After several months, the authorities decided to keep the area intact and improve the facilities with a modern electric cable system and private restrooms.

In Shanghai you can still find some renovated Shikumen. The most famous one is Xintiandi, which is a perfect combination of traditional Chinese architecture with Western influence. This area is becoming a key tourist attraction in Shanghai and is adjacent to the luxury shopping malls in Huaihai Lu. Unfortunately, however, nothing there has retained its past glory other than the building structure.

The architecture of the Shikumen is similar to that of Moroccan houses. They both have Riad main entrances and contain few floors, and all the rooms in each type of house are linked to the courtyard, where they have access to natural light and fresh air.

比如他母亲一大早要在街上冲洗一个老式的红木桶。这个桶装过一家大小的粪便。他母亲总是在小巷外等着马车来收粪便，与一同等待的邻居闲聊。那时，家家户户都是这样子。红木桶是中国的传统物件，它常被用作送给新婚夫妇的礼物，有时桶里会放一些钱和物品。

几年前，在世博会以前，他的房子和这一带的其他房子都曾面临着拆迁。问题是如果房子才拆了，哪里又有地方安置这么多的人呢？经过几个月的考虑，政府决定保留这些房子，还对这个区的基础设施进行了改造，更新了供电系统，增建私人卫生间。

现在，在上海，你还是能找到一些整修过的石库门建筑。最著名的是新天地，所有那里的商铺，展现出中国传统与西方影响的完美结合范例。毗邻淮海路的高级商业街，这个地方已经成为最受欢迎的上海景点之一。

仅建筑结构而言，没有什么比石库门更有上海味了。

石库门建筑真的很接近带着里亚德式入口的摩洛哥建筑。楼层和所有的房间都连接庭院，有更好的自然采光和新鲜空气。

The traditional Muslim Market making a comeback

传统穆斯林市场去而复返

The Muslim market is the perfect example of Shanghai as a multicultural Megalopolis where you can find different cultures, religions and, of course, hundreds of types of food. I used to recommend that my customers enjoy some of the authentic Chinese food sold on that street.

This is my favorite area, not because of the ambiance, but because it reminds me of my Mediterranean roots in Armenia, where my grandfather was born.

The market-style atmosphere was enlivened by the smell of spices, people shouting, screaming, enjoying a coffee or a mint, and smoking the Shisha which brought me back to the memories of the time with my mother's side of the family and also time when I was in Lebanon.

Thanks to this market near the Jing'an's Huxi Mosqie, you feel the pride of the Uighur Muslim minorities for their culinary culture. The local Uighur minorities who have settled in Shanghai gather at the bazaar to share their Jumu'ah (Friday prayer) and break bread together.

Meat, spices, pastries, dry nuts and fruits are exhibited on traditional stalls. Butchers cut mutton in the street, barbecued kebab are smoking, the mint tea supplier makes a show of pouring tea into a cup from a teapot a meter above, woks crackle with rice pilaf, the heavy smell of deep-fried pastries covered with honey permeates the air, and so much more.

I detected the same scents I smelled when I used to go with my grandfather to the Oriental shop in Paris: olives, pastries, dates, pistachios, salami, and candy fruit. It's a part of my culinary heritage from my mother.

But this whole atmosphere almost disappeared last May, 2013, when the local authorities decided to relocate this market to another district, due to neighborhood complaints.

The reasons were practical rather than political, caused by things like the noises, smoke, smells, and traffic from the market.

在我看来，要证明上海是一个多元文化的国际大都市，穆斯林市场就是一个完美的范例。你能在上海找到不同文化、地区元素，当然，还有成百上千种食物。我曾推荐不少我的顾客去这里的街边常常真正的中国美食。

这个地方是我的最爱，不是因为它的周边环境，而是因为它让我想起我地中海的祖辈文化根源。我外祖父是亚美尼亚人。

这个市场的样式气氛，香料味萦绕，人们吆喝、大笑，品着咖啡或薄荷，吸着阿拉伯水烟……所有这些，把我带回母亲那一脉的家族记忆，也让我想起曾在黎巴嫩的日子。

由于这个市场，你能够感觉到维吾尔少数民族在静安沪西清真寺附近展示他们烹饪文化的骄傲。维吾尔少数民族

After this short interruption - the "power" of the Chinese street food is in a constant state of flux in Shanghai - the market returned with a few changes. Some stalls were moved back to the Mosque so as not to interfere with traffic. And of course, out of respect for each other, the stall owners were expected to keep their market on track.

The Muslim market is not the only area in Shanghai where you can find street food.

The best time of year is National day - from the 1st to the 4th of October. At that occasion,

many artisans from the countryside bring their own neighborhood street food. You can get any kind of food there: Muslim, Chinese, Taiwanese, or Hong Kong.

Nanjing Lu, one of the main streets in downtown Shanghai, is packed with this food, as are areas like Yuyuan garden, Wujian Lu, Yunnan Lu, Huanghe Lu, and Qibao.

Each area in town has its own street food specifications. Some sell snacks, others hot pot, seafood, dumplings.

If you want to enjoy almost every variety of street food you can get in Shanghai, you

聚居在上海这个集市附近，共度主麻日（周五祈祷），一起进餐。

传统小摊上，琳琅满目摆放着肉类、香料、点心、干果、坚果。屠夫在街上割羊肉，烧烤摊上冒着烟，薄荷茶小贩表演着从一米高倒茶的功夫，香肉饭在铁锅里滋滋作响，浇着蜂蜜的油炸点心散发着浓烈香气……太多太多了。

在这里我感受到曾经和外祖父在巴黎东方商店中一模一样的气味，橄榄、甜点、枣子、开心果、意大利腊肠、糖果、水果……各种香气将我拉回童年的记忆。这是我从母亲那继承的烹饪基因的一部分。

但在 2013 年，即去年 5 月，所有这些都几乎消失了。附近几个居民区投诉，政府决定把集市迁出这个区。这不是因为政治因素，而更多是出于吵闹、烟雾、气味、交通拥堵的考虑。然而，中国街边食物总是流动而生命强大的。短时间的中断后，集市带着些许变化，回复正常。一些摊位移回了清真寺，不那么妨碍交通，当然也更尊重彼此，从而维持着集市的生存运转。

穆斯林集市不是上海唯一让你找到街边食物的地方。一年中最好的时刻是国庆节 10 月 1 日到 4 日。这个时候，

许多工匠从乡村带来他们家乡的街边小食。你能在穆斯林、中国内地、台湾、香港商家那儿找到任何一种食物。南京路，上海市中心主要的一条街道，可以吃到各式小吃。要品尝小吃，你还可以去豫园、吴江路、云南路、黄河路和七宝镇等。

每条街还有各自的美食特色。有些

should go to Qibao. It is the first water town near downtown Shanghai and easily accessible by metro. Qibao is a long street full of small souvenir shops, restaurants, snacks, artwork, and sculptures. Most of the Shanghainese people go there during the weekend to enjoy the many varieties of snacks.

I found so many goodies: chicken cooked in clay (jiaohuaji in the nipa), skewered birds, dumplings, fried seafood, quail eggs cooked in rock salt, rice steamed in bamboo, plus countless other delicacies.

One interesting thing I discovered in a small lane behind the main street was an unexpected monument - a catholic church, (Church of the Assumption of Mary) built in 1866.

The priest invited me to join the evening prayer. It was my first time to take part in the prayer in Chinese, but most of the time everybody were singing in English. This event provided a short moment of tranquility in the midst of a busy and crowded trip.

Street food memories

An Oyster omelet is simply cooked on the teppanyaki with eggs, chopped Chinese cabbage, spring onions, oysters and wasabi powder. It is a gorgeous dish - slightly spicy and sticky with a strong oyster flavor.

Enjoying the crayfish in Xishan road with a 3 Michelin stars Pascal Bardot was a unique experience. It was almost 2 p.m. when we went in a malodorous street shop to enjoy some crayfish. The crayfish was outstanding simply steamed or with a touch of soy sauce and chili oil. It was an honor to spend this time with the team of a famous Michelin star chef. If you want to enjoy excellent crayfish, I recommend Chongming island, where you can eat it from the organic farms. Their meat is both tastier and safer.

The traditional spring onions crepe used to be eaten by laborers before they started their hard day's work. The choice of street food is a personal taste, but you can't go wrong if you follow the locals. If the place is packed – even if it is not very clean - it means that the food is outstanding and you are sure to enjoy it.

街全卖小吃，种类繁多，有火锅、海鲜和水饺等。

如果你想找个地方把上海街边美食一一尝遍，不妨去七宝镇。这是临近市中心的第一个水乡，坐地铁很容易到的。一条长长的街道，满是纪念品店、饭店、小吃、艺术品、雕塑。

大多数上海人周末去那里，品尝各种小吃。我发现那儿种类是如此丰富，有用泥土包裹着做的鸡，叫做叫花鸡，烧烤鸟肉，饺子，油炸海鲜，岩盐里的鹌鹑蛋，竹筒米饭……

我还在一条主要街道的小巷后，意想不到地发现一块纪念碑，一座建于1866年的天主教堂（圣母升天堂）。牧师邀请我加入晚间祷告，这是我第一次在中国参加祷告。但多数时候，每个人都在那儿用英语唱，歌声带来了人群中宁静的片刻。

街边美食的回忆

铁板烧上简单烹饪的牡蛎蛋卷，材料有鸡蛋、碎白菜、香葱、牡蛎和芥末粉，好吃极了。有一点辣，牡蛎味儿很浓。

和米其林三星大厨 Pascal Bardot 一起，品尝西山路小龙虾是一次很特别的经历。差不多下午 2 点我们走进一条气味难闻的街道，享受小龙虾。简单蒸熟，蘸点酱油、辣椒油，味道棒极了。能和一个著名的米其林星级厨师一起在街边小吃档共享美好时光，感觉很特别。

如果你想吃上好小龙虾，更推荐你去崇明岛。那里有机农场的小龙虾，不但味道更佳，而且更安全。让人印象深刻的小吃还有传统的香葱薄饼，过去是工人们开始一天劳作前吃的。僻静之地的鱼头饭店，或者小巷垃圾区后的老牌面店也总有惊喜不断。

选择街边食物，要根据自己的口味。不过想做出正确的选择，你必须总跟着当地人。如果一个地方尽管不很干净，却食客盈门，这说明这个地方东西很好吃，你也肯定会喜欢。

精雕王
19.50元
五年陈花雕
5.80元
三年陈
2.70元
咸亨酒

Recipe 14
食谱 14

red wild chongming crayfish, watercress puree, and cumin ginger sauce
崇明野生小龙虾，配西洋菜泥和孜然姜汁

4 Servings

4 人份

Ingredients
配料

400 g ---------------------------------- Wild crayfish 野生小龙虾

Broth
汤

100 g -- Onion 洋葱

80 g -- Carrot 胡萝卜

30 Kg --- Celery 西芹

750 ml -- Water 水

750 ml --- White wine 白酒

4 --- Egg yolk 蛋黄

Watercress puree
西洋菜泥

700 g --- Watercress 西洋菜

Emulsion
乳液

50 g --- Sour cream 酸奶油

100 ml -- Milk 牛奶

50 ml -- White vinegar 白醋

100 ml ---------------------------------- Crayfish broth 小龙虾汤

Cumin sauce
孜然汁

200 ml -- Soy sauce 酱油

5 g -- Cumin powder 孜然粉

100 g -- Water chestnut 马蹄

10 g --- Ginger 姜

Directions
作法

1. Broth:

a. Dice the vegetables in 0.5 cm cubes; put them in a sauce pan and add the water and wine.

b. Cook for 30 minutes.

c. Strain, keep the vegetables. Keep the broth warm.

d. Clean the crayfish and poach them in the broth for 2 minutes. Take 500 ml of the broth and add the egg yolks. Cook slowly till it is like a custard cream.

汤：a. 把蔬菜切成 0.5 厘米的小丁，放入锅里，加水和酒。

b. 煮 30 分钟。

c. 收汁，留下蔬菜，保持汤汁是热的。

d. 清洗小龙虾，用浓汤煮 2 分钟，取 0.5 升的汤，加入蛋黄。慢煮成乳蛋奶油状。

2. Watercress puree:

a. Clean the watercress and keep only the leaves. Blanch them in salty water and cool them down in ice water.

b. Blend them together; strain and add the crayfish broth.

西洋菜泥：a. 清洗并留些叶子，用盐水灼，后用冰水冷却。

b. 搅拌，收汁，加入小龙虾汤。

3. Emulsion:

Mix 100 ml broth with the milk and the cream. Taste the seasoning and add the white vinegar. Keep it in the fridge and before it's done, use the blender to make the emulsion.

乳液：用牛奶和奶油混入 100 毫升的汤里，调味并添加白醋，放入冰箱存放，最后一分钟用搅拌器制成乳状汤。

4. Garnish:

In the small bowl pour the watercress cream, put one crayfish and sprinkle with the diced veggies, pour on top the emulsion.

装饰：把西洋菜奶油倒入小碗中，放一个小龙虾并撒些蔬菜丁，在顶上倒些乳状汤。

5. Cumin sauce:

a. Heat the soy sauce and add the cumin powder; Add the ginger julienne.

b. Slice the water chestnuts and boil them.

孜然汁：a. 加热酱油并放入孜然粉，添加姜丝。

b. 把马蹄切片并煮熟。

6. Set up:

Pour the watercress puree at the bottom of a plate. Add the crayfish, the head, then the emulsion and the cumin sauce.

You can add some fresh herbs if you like.

摆盘：把西洋菜泥放在底部，放上小龙虾，头，然后倒入乳液和孜然汁。可根据个人口味添加新鲜的香草。

Your notes

Great recipes are not created, but perfected.
好的食谱来自一次又一次的修改完善。

Note down the changes you make on this recipe to create your very own version of it.
记录下你对这个食谱做的修改，探寻属于你自己的味道。

Chef's tips
厨师贴士

If it's not the season of the crayfish you can make a similar recipe with some big river shrimps or langoustine from the sea.

如果不是小龙虾季节，你可以使用一些大的河虾或海虾，例如来海螯虾来做这个食谱。

15

故事十五

Lands and Green Spaces

上海绿地与特别区域

Green spaces in Shanghai are utilized in a similar manner compared to those in western countries. The parks are free spaces where all the social classes share a common area. You can find kids playing sports, elderly people chatting around a cup of tea, card-playing, sleeping, relaxing, dancing, musicians playing instruments, painting and practically anything else you can imagine. The main difference between western parks and parks in Shanghai is that the park is more often employed for the well-being of the body. Chinese seniors often practice Tai Chi early in the morning, and engage in other forms of physical exercise. However, the younger generation is much less attentive to these things.

One of the best areas in downtown Shanghai to find all of these aspects of life is in LuXun Park.

The first time I had been there was almost 3 years ago. I went there with a friend who wanted to show me where the Chinese people go to swim - in the public pond. This was an unusual concept for me, but I followed them and went swimming in a dirty public pond in downtown Shanghai. A huge sign cited, "Swimming not allowed". Here was another Chinese paradox – that which is forbidden is often tolerated.

Lu Xun Park - formerly Hongkou Park - is an urban park in the Hongkou District of Shanghai, the People's Republic of China. The park is located on 146 East Jiangwan Road, right behind the Hongkou Stadium.

The municipality initiated the construction of a shooting range for international commercial groups. Following the style of sports parks in Glasgow, United Kingdom, and designed by a British garden designer, it was christened Hongkou Amusement Park. In 1905, it was rebuilt as "Hongkou Sports Games Park and Shooting Field. Finally, in 1922, it was simply renamed "Hongkou Park".

上海绿地利用方式与西方国家差不多。公园是所有社会阶层共享的免费空间。孩子们运动，老年人喝茶聊天，打牌，睡觉，放松，跳舞，音乐人弹奏乐器，绘画……你可以想象的几乎任何活动。上海公园和西方国家公园的主要区别是，上海的公园更经常用于锻炼身体。中国老年人经常在清晨打太极和做其他形式的体育锻炼。但年轻一代并不太关注这些。

在上海市区，鲁迅公园是这些日常活动最活跃的地方之一。我第一次来这里是在大约三年前。我和一个朋友一起，他想带我看看中国人游泳的地方。那是一个公共池塘，这对我来说真是不同寻常的概念。但我还是跟着他们，在这个肮脏的上海市区公共池塘里游了泳。那有一个巨大的标识，写着“禁止游泳”。然而，这是中国另一个悖论—那些明令禁止的东西，往往会被宽容。

鲁迅公园，原称“虹口公园”，是中华人民共和国上海虹口区的一个城市公园。公园坐落在东江湾路 146 号，虹口体育场背后。它最初是上海市政府为国际商业团体营建的射击场，风格上参照英国格拉斯哥运动公园，由英国园林设计师设计，命名为虹口游乐园。1905 年，它被重建为“虹口体育比赛公园和靶场”。最后，在 1922 年，简单更名为“虹口公园”。

Jewish district, still standing Hongkou district

犹太区，依旧矗立在虹口区

After several years in Shanghai I finally learned that the Jewish district was just not far from the Bund.

I got the chance to visit this area with a group of Jews from all around the world. Most of them have their own family story tracing back to their grandparents during the Second World War. The leader of this visit was Dvir Bar-Gal from Israel.

This man had an amazing personal story. He came to Shanghai several decades ago and, in short, decided to find the Jewish cemetery where all the ancestors' graves still exist.

But in the last decades Shanghai's landscape had changed dramatically, and the graves had been moved to the Foreigner's cemetery in the city suburbs.

After years of research, testimonies, and the support of the local people, many tombstones have been discovered on the road, near houses, in ponds, and even being used as a washboard for clothes.

The older generation of villagers had no idea about the significances of the Hebrew writing or of the star of David, so no one paid attention to that.

But thanks to the dedication of certain men, the Israeli consulate and the Chinese authorities are slowly recovering these tombstones.

在上海待了几年，我才知道在外滩不远的地方有个犹太区。

我拜访这一地区是与一群来自世界各地的犹太人一起。他们大多数都有自己的家庭故事。发生在第二次世界大战期间，他们祖父母一代的故事。这次访问的领导者是来自以色列的 Dvir Bar-Gal。

这人有了不起的亲身经历。几十年前，他来到上海。然后，简单说就是，他决定寻找先辈们的犹太公墓。但在过去几十年，上海城市地貌发生了翻天覆地的变化，坟墓都已纷纷迁往城郊外国人墓地。

经过多年研究、听取意见，在当地人支持下，许多墓碑被找了出来。发现时，它们在路上、在房子旁边，在池塘里，甚至被用作搓衣板。

老一辈村民不识希伯来文，也不懂犹太“大卫之星”，所以没有人注意到这些墓碑。

现在，由于信徒的捐献，以色列领事馆和中国当局在慢慢修复这些墓碑。

The ghetto saved from destruction
犹太区免于毁灭

In 2009, many old areas in Shanghai needed to be renovated or destroyed for the world expo. The Jewish ghetto was one of the areas on the list, as the municipality hoped to expand road access into this region. But the city decided to preserve this district and develop a Jewish museum to remind present and future generations of what happened in Shanghai in previous decades.

Now, only Chinese people live in the formerly Jewish ghetto, and only a few elements remain to remind you of the existence of this Jewish community.

In terms of food - contrary to the strong influence of Muslim food in other parts of China - kosher food did not make a big impact in Shanghai. There are few kosher shops and Sino-Jewish cuisine doesn't exist. A culinary experience would be interesting to develop here.

2009 年，为迎接世博会，上海很多老区需要翻新或拆除。由于市政府想拓宽进入这一地区的道路，犹太聚集区也进了拆除名单之列。但最终还是决定保留，于是成立了一个犹太博物馆，希望告诉现在和以后的人们，几十年前这里曾发生的故事。

现在，只有中国人生活在先前的犹太聚居区，也只有少数元素仍提醒你这里曾是犹太社区。

食物方面的话，与中国其他地区穆斯林食物的强大影响力不同，犹太食品在上海没什么影响。几乎没有犹太商店，“中国犹太菜”根本不存在。发展这一块的话，进行一次烹饪体验会很有趣。

The Story of Xialongbao

小笼包的故事

Generally thought to have been invented in the late 19th century - possibly as early as the years preceding the Guang Xu period (1875-1908) of Qing China - xiao long bao hail from the town of Nan Xiang in what is now Shanghai's Jiading district.

There, they are called xiao long man tou ("little basket steamed bread"). As the rumor goes, the first XLB were sold out of a shop owned by a Mr. Huang Mingxian, who was driven to innovate them due to the increased competition of new vendors attracted to the crowds his famous steamed buns brought in. The similar shape of Yangzhou tang bao (soup buns) to XLB indicates they may have also originated from Mr. Huang, though they are much larger. It's unlikely, however, that he invented both breads on his own.

Two specialist xiaolongbao restaurants have had particularly long histories. One is Nanxiang Mantou Dian (Nanxiang Bun Shop). This shop resulted from the original store in Nanxiang, but is now located in the City God Temple precinct. It is famed for its crab-meat-filled buns. The other is Gulong Restaurant, which can be found at the original site next to Guyi Garden in Nanxiang.

Xiaolongbao are traditionally filled with pork, but variations include other meat, seafood and vegetarian fillings. One popular variety is pork with minced crabmeat and roe. The

一般认为，小笼包是发明于 19 世纪晚期—可能早于清光绪年间 (1875 – 1908)。小笼包起源在南翔镇，也就是现在的上海嘉定区之内。那里，它们被称为“小笼馒头”。传说，小笼包最早是一个叫黄明贤的人经营的店铺出售的。他发明小笼包，是为了应对同行激烈的竞争压力。扬州汤包体积更大一点，但与小笼包形状差不多，外形上似乎暗示都是黄先生的发明，但似乎不太可能都是他一个人发明的。

在上海，专做小笼包的老字号有两家。一家是南翔馒头店（南翔包子店）。这家店起源自原始的南翔店铺，但现在位于城隍庙区。它出名的是蟹肉包。另

characteristic soup-filled kind is created by wrapping solid meat aspic inside the skin together with the meat filling.

Traditionally the xiaolongbao is a kind of dim sum or snack item. The Chinese word for this type of snack is "xiaochi" which, literally translated, means "small eat". The buns are served hot in the bamboo baskets they were steamed in, usually on a bed of dried leaves or on a woven mat - although some restaurants today use napa cabbage instead. The buns are generally dipped in Chinkiang vinegar with shredded ginger, and are often served with a clear soup.

Modern Variations

The Xialongbao is highly appreciated by westerners and tourists. You can experiment with the flavors of the filling and the broth until they suit your personal tastes.

Many Chinese chefs are using some western ingredients in the filling to make a Sino "Laowai" version. Goose Liver and black truffle are two common substitutes. I have customized my cooking to adapt to the palates of many of my international patrons.

- French

Beef Bourguignon, Boiled beef "Pot au Feu", Burgundy snails

Lemon tart, Bittersweet chocolate, Strawberry

- Swiss

Swiss cheese fondue, Porcini cheese

Swiss chocolate fondue

- Italian

Minestrone soup, Margarita pizza, Mozzarella, Tiramisu

- Thai

Red duck curry, Tom Yum Kung

Coconut, Lemongrass

All of these variations are achievable, but you must take into consideration two factors: the filling must contain a liquid, and the skin has to be thicker to prevent the wrap from melting quickly containing the liquid.

一家是古龙饭庄，在紧挨着南翔古猗园的原始地点。

小笼包传统是猪肉馅，但也用别的肉类、海鲜和素食做馅。一个流行的品种是把猪肉、切碎的蟹肉和鱼子混和做馅。特色汤汁，用面皮裹着肉皮冻与碎肉。

传统上，小笼包是一种点心或零食。中文把这种类型的零食称为“小吃”，从字面上翻译，意味着“少量的或小的吃食”。包子热乎乎地端上桌，以蒸熟它的竹制篮筐为盛器，通常下面垫着干叶或编织垫—尽管一些餐馆现在用卷心菜。小笼包一般蘸镇江醋和姜丝吃，通常还配有一个清汤。

现代的小笼包创新

小笼包很受中外游客欢迎。做小笼包，你可以不断试验采用不同馅和汤汁，直到你找到合适你个人口味的馅料。为了做出一个适合老外吃的版本，许多中国厨师在馅里加入西方配料，例如鹅肝和黑松露。我也根据餐厅顾客的要求设计了几款适应不同国家人群口味的小笼包。

· 法国口味

红酒炖牛肉、“蔬菜炖牛肉火上锅”、勃艮第蜗牛、柠檬馅饼、苦甜巧克力、草莓

· 瑞士口味

瑞士奶酪、牛肝菌奶酪、瑞士巧克力火锅

· 意大利口味

意大利蔬菜汤，玛格丽塔披萨、马苏里拉奶酪、提拉米苏

· 泰国口味

红咖喱鸭、冬阴功汤、椰子、柠檬草

要做这几种口味的小笼包不算困难，但你必须考虑两个因素：包子馅必须有汤液，同时面皮厚一点，来避免面皮在包裹汤汁时轻易融化。

Recipe 15
食谱 15

nanxiang crab xiao long bao
南翔蟹肉小笼包

6 Servings
6 人份

Ingredients
配料

1 kg	Flour 面粉
150 g	Cornstarch 生粉
150 g	Water chestnut flour 马蹄粉
150 g	Bread flour 高筋面粉
500 g	Butter crab 黄油蟹
100 g	Pork belly 五花肉
100 g	Red crab roe 红蟹籽
200 g	Water 水

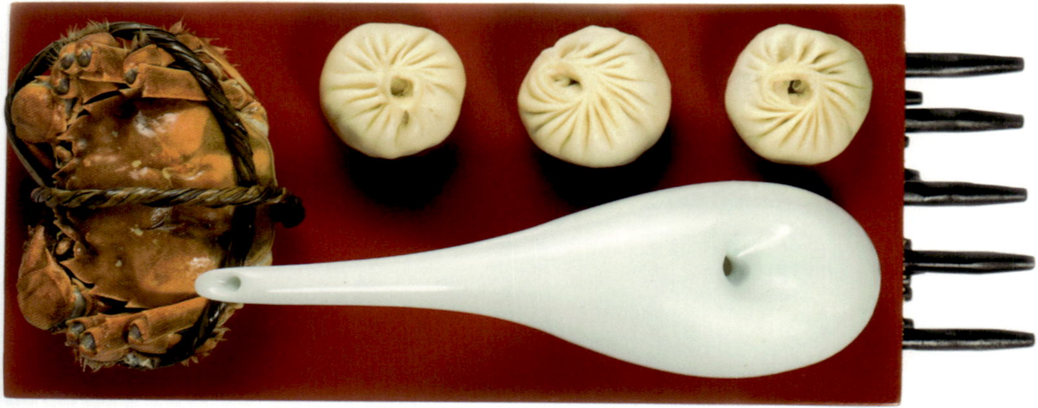

Directions
作法

1. Mix the flour with the water to make the dough and let it sit for 30 minutes.

先将所有面粉搅拌成面团，静置 30 分钟。

2. Cut the pork belly in cube1 cm side. Add some salt and sugar in the crab meat to make the filling.

将五花肉切成每边 1 厘米的粒，加入盐和糖搅拌好再加入黄油蟹肉弄成馅。

3. Get a small ball from the paste, each ball is 15 g in weight. Press the ball to be thin and add the filling in the middle. Wrap it and give it a fish mouth shape.

将面团出体每粒重 15 克，开薄包入馅料，弄成鱼嘴型。

4. Steam for 7 minutes. Add some crab roe on the top of the bun to serve.

加热 7 分钟后取出，在鱼嘴处加入红蟹籽即可。

16

故事十六

Living in Shanghai

上海生活

The People's Square is a large public square in the Huangpu District of Shanghai. It is on the south of Nanjing Road (West) and north of Huaihai Road (East). People's Square is the site of Shanghai's municipal government headquarters, and has been used as the standard reference point for measurement of distance in the city.

Prior to 1949 and the establishment of the People's Republic of China, what is now People's Square was a place for horse racing owned by the Shanghai Race Club. After gambling and horse racing were banned by the new Communist government, a part of the race course became the People's Square, which included a large avenue and spectator stands for use during parades.

In the 1990s, major changes were made to the square. The Shanghai Municipal Government and the Shanghai Museum were both relocated here from their former residences at the HSBC Building in the Bund and a former office building respectively. More recent additions include the Shanghai Grand Theatre and the Shanghai Urban Planjning Exhibition Hall.

人民广场是上海黄埔区大型公共广场。它在南京路以南，淮海路以北。人民广场是上海市政府所在地，并用作城市测量距离的标准参考点。

1949 年中华人民共和国成立前，现在人民广场所在的地方是上海跑马总会举行赛马的场所。共产党新政府禁止赌博和赛马后，赛马场的一部分成为了人民广场，其中包括一条宽阔街道和游行阅兵时的观众看台。

1990 年代，广场的规划发生了很多的变化。上海市政府和上海博物馆分别从外滩的汇丰银行大厦和另一座办公大楼迁移至此。近年成立的还有上海大剧院和上海城市规划展示馆。

People's Square, "Blind date corner"

人民广场的"相亲角"

The marriage market at People's Square has existed since 2004.

It is a place where parents of unmarried adults gather, desperately trying to marry off their single offspring every Saturday and Sunday from noon to 5 p.m.

The primary goal of attending the Shanghai marriage market is for parents to find a suitable partner for their child.

The standards of finding the right match may be based upon

-Age (Yet, age doesn't really matter that much anymore.)

-Height (men must be taller than women)

-Job

-Incomes

-Education (the trend: the partner has studied abroad)

-Family values

-Chinese zodiac sign

-Personality

(Physical appearance is not important)

All of this information is written on a piece of paper, which is then hung on long strings among other parents' advertisements for their children. The parents walk around chatting with other parents to see if there is a harmonious fit, but only after their children's' standards are met.

Many parents do not have permission from their child to go to this event.

In many parents' eyes, matchmaking gatherings such as the Shanghai Marriage Market are the only way to uphold a traditional dating style for their children in modern China. China's long idealized tradition of continuing their family lineage is very important within Chinese culture.

This tradition is still observed by some rich western families, the Indians, people in some African countries and Arabic countries. A common underlying reason is to preserve some traditions and their social status.

An important statistic to remember is that in 2020, 24 million marriageable men will not be able to find a spouse. This figure does not account for foreign men who marry Chinese women, divorces (4 million per year), and also concubines who are back "on the market " for several years. (This was a tradition for a length of time in China)

Recently, well-educated women in China with established careers are less anxious to get married. They have more options than women in past generations and are not afraid to give priority to their careers. This change in marriage ideology puts women in a higher position of power within a traditionally male-dominated society. Now, more women seek to find a responsible man with personal integrity instead of just a high-paying job.

Back to the market, some men go to extreme lengths to get the attention of their desired

人民广场的婚姻市场最初在 2004 年开始出现。

这里每逢周六日的中午到下午 5 点，都会聚集许多未婚成年人的父母。他们都使尽浑身解数，想要帮各自的单身儿女找到合适的对象。

在这个"相亲角"，他们一般遵循的配偶标准有：

—年龄（但是似乎现在年龄对他们来说已经没那么重要了）

—身高（男方必须比女方高）

—工作

—收入

—教育(现在留过学的比较受欢迎)

—家庭价值观

—生肖属相

—性格

（外表并不是特别重要）

他们会把这些信息写在一张纸上，写完了挂在一条长绳上，这条长绳还挂满了父母们为儿女制作的征婚广告。我就曾亲自看到过一对父母和另一对父母边散步聊天边探讨各自的儿女是否符合彼此的要求。

许多父母没有经过子女的允许就参加这样的一个"相亲角"。时至今日，在很多父母眼中，想要守住"父母之命，媒妁之言"的中国传统婚配模式，像上海婚姻市场这样的相亲聚会是唯一的途径。延续家族血脉的悠久理想化传统，在中国文化中占据着重要地位。

遵守这个传统的还有一些富裕的西方家庭、印度人、一些非洲国家和阿拉伯国家的人。他们这样做，一个深层的

partner's family members, including donning the trendiest exotic clothing. Some parents even strike deals with other parents to find a suitable match. I have seen of these agreements first hand. My friend met with a Chinese family who was willing to pay up to 7,000 U.S. dollars just for the contact information of a foreign expatriate. This man was French, single, and also a financial trader in Shanghai with a handsome salary, the perfect combination for a respected family.

For any foreigner to be considered, you must first be good looking, but even that factor will not guarantee your success. Your wallet is more important. The values held deepest by the Chinese differ from those in the West. More of an emphasis is placed on financial security and lifestyle rather than feelings of love and attachment.

共同原因是为了保留一些传统，并维持他们的社会地位。

到 2020 年，将有 2400 万适婚男性无法找到配偶。这个数字还没算上与外国人结婚的中国女性（中国人与外国人离婚的每年就有四百万之多），也没算上近年来重回婚姻市场的情妇们（中国一夫多妻的传统由来已久）。

近年，受过良好教育、建立了个人事业的中国女性也不急于结婚。与过去几代人相比，现代中国女性有更多选择，有条件去优先考虑自己的事业。婚姻观念的这种变化，使得女性在一个传统的男权社会中有了更高的位置。现在，更多的女性会想找一个品行正直、负责任的伴侣，而不是盲目地给自己找一张高额度的长期饭票。

回到婚姻市场的话题。一些男性不得不全力以赴去获得心上人家庭成员的关注，这包括，套上时髦的外国潮衣。为找匹配对象，一些父母甚至与其他父母达成各种有几分荒谬的协议。我看过第一手的协议。我朋友遇到过一个中国家庭，这家人愿意出价 7000 美元来买一个外籍人士的联系方式。这是个是法国人，单身，在上海做过金融交易员，收入可观，对一个受人尊敬的家庭而言，他是个完美的结婚对象。

如果一个外国人想要得到这些中国家长的青睐，首先，你的长相很重要，但就是这个因素也不能确保你的成功，你的经济实力也很重要。与西方社会区别很大的一点是，中国家庭把经济上的生活保障看得很重要。总体给人的感觉是爱情的热烈心跳和两性的吸引根本比不过家境宽裕的条件。

The Antique market Dong Tai lu

东台路古玩市场

According to historical records, Dongtai Road was built in the year 1902, during the reign of Emperor Guangxu of the Qing Dynasty. At that time it was named Taishan Road.

In 1906, it was named Rue Hennequin after an official in the former French Concession. In 1943 it was finally named Dongtai Road and the name is still used today.

In the very beginning, this road was actually a place where people would drink morning tea and have breakfast. Chinese people have been fond of collecting antiques and curios since ancient times. Many customers who came here for tea or breakfast would also bring their own collections, exchange ideas, or swap artifacts. Some antique shops began to appear and gradually Dongtai Road became a gathering place for antique shops and stands.

This street is now full of sellers who sell copies of notable antiques and pieces of Chinese history, such as sculptures, artwork, crafts, and souvenirs.

I often went there to find some ideas for decorating the hotel where I was working. The plethora of antiques, both art deco and Asian style, offer an array of choices.

You can find different items at a wide range of prices. You must always keep in mind if you decide to invest in expensive antiques, then you should have no issue spending a large amount. Furniture or vases are not cheap.

Foreigners still think Chinese antiques are cheap and they feel satisfied when they find a bargain, but for anything in China you must remember one important thing-

YOU GET WHAT YOU PAY FOR.

Everyone looks for the best deal, but for everything, even clothing, you must pay a certain price to purchase an item of decent quality.

On Dongtai Lu the best time to deal is in the middle of the afternoon when the sellers start to become exhausted from the day's work. The encounter is not always easy and it depends what you are searching for. Some sellers own unique pieces so they can set their own fixed prices with little room to bargain. Even after haggling for upwards of thirty minutes, the result is sometimes less than favorable. My wife once spent more than one hour to negotiate the price of a marble elephant statue, not even an antique but of good quality and quite appealing.

If you buy a true antique in China (meaning it pre-dates 1949), then you must secure a certificate and requisite stamps from the Shanghai Relics Bureau before taking it out of the country. These include items dating from 1796-1949. Any artifacts from the era before 1795 are forbidden from leaving China without exception.

Places for antique shopping

1. Hu & Hu, No. 8, Lane 1885 Cao Bao Lu. Antiques

For a reliable selection of legitimate antiques and reproductions from a dealer who does not scam people on either quality or price, Marybelle Hu is your lady. With fourteen years of experience, Hu has the know-how and the connections to source some amazing pieces and her warehouse is a great place to find unique antiques or made-to-measure reproductions.

2. Art Deco on Dongtai Lu

One of our all time favorite Shanghai shopping experiences of any kind lies behind Dongtai Lu. Antique market stalls overflow with mostly kitschy curios. A number of these stores specialize in Shanghai art deco pieces at reasonable and somewhat negotiable prices. Two particularly good ones are called Shanghai Art Deco and Modern Shanghai.

3. Ze Casa 558 Feng Hua Gong Lu, near Xin Fu Lu

Another excellent option for top quality Shanghai art deco pieces, made from 1910 to 1950, is Ze Casa. This period of craftsmanship in Shanghai produced distinct pieces, different from the art deco seen elsewhere because of the influence of traditional Chinese motifs, such as cranes and flowers. The prices here are higher than at the less carefully curated locations around town, but they are commensurate with the quality, which is second to none.

4. Green Antiques 4877 Jiasong Zhong Lu

Green Antiques is a giant 100,000 square foot warehouse filled with antiques from a variety of locales and time periods. There really is a huge selection of offerings here. Make sure you allow plenty of time for exploration, as the sheer amount of products can be overwhelming.

5. Shanghai Mu Lan Hua Ge Jia Ju Li Curio Company, 1788 Ji Yang Lu, near Shangpu Lu

Some people prefer their antique shopping to be a sanitary experience, involving beautiful spaces and carefully curated collections. If you are one of those people, steer clear of this place, which is as messy as its name is long-winded. This giant clearing warehouse has 20-meter high piles of furniture: trunks, chairs, tables, ladders, stools and Buddha statues galore, all for highly negotiable prices. Dig through the multitudes of rubbish to find your dream antique pieces and curios, then allow one of the friendly fellows who staff the warehouse to clean it up before delivering it to your home.

根据历史记载，东台路始建于1902年，清朝光绪皇帝统治期间。当时它被命名为泰山路。1906年，它又以一个法租界官员的名字命名，叫纳金路。1943年，最终取名东台路，并沿用至今。

一开始，这条路其实是人们喝早茶、吃早点的地方。中国人自古以来就喜爱收集古董珍奇。很多来这里喝茶、吃早点的顾客会带上自己的收藏，交换想法或者交易物件。一些古董店开始出现，东台路逐渐成为了古董商店和摊位的聚集地。

如今这里满大街的商家都出售著名古董仿制品和刻画中国历史的物件，比如雕塑、艺术品、工艺品和纪念品等。

我经常去那里找灵感，想着怎样装饰我工作的酒店。品类繁多的古董，富含装饰艺术，满是亚洲风情，为我提供了大量选择。价格有高有低，各类古玩应有尽有。你必须始终牢记，如果你决定买什么昂贵的古董，你也要狠下心来愿意花很多钱，家具或花瓶并不便宜。

外国人仍然认为中国古董便宜。讨价还价拿到了折扣，他们觉得满足。但对于在中国的一切，你必须记住重要的一点—你付多少钱，你得到怎样的东西。每个人都寻找最好的交易，但对一切，甚至平常一件衣服，你也得花一定价钱才能买件品质像样的。

在东台路交易的最佳时间是下午的中间时段。大半天工作下来，卖家已经开始疲倦了。过程并不总是很轻松，主要还取决于你正在寻找的是什么。一些卖家有自己的独特品，他们可以设定固定价格，几乎没什么讨价还价的余地。有时甚至讨价还价了半个多小时，结果也不尽如人意。我妻子就曾花一个多小时为一个大理石大象雕塑讨价还价，这雕像甚至不是个古董，仅是质量上乘，造型吸引罢了。

如果你在中国买一个真古董（意思是它的年代早于1949年），带离出境前，你必须有一个证书，并且在上海文物局盖过章。你买的古董年份要在1796到1949年间。1795年以前的文物一律不准带离中国。

买古董的好去处

1. 胡胡店，漕宝路1885弄8号。

买合法古董和仿制品，找一个既不在质量上、也不在价格上欺诈你的商家，胡女士是一个可靠选择。十四年的行业经验，胡女士有着丰富的古玩知识，也有获得非凡珍品的渠道，她的仓库里存储了很多独特的古玩，也提供高仿品的定制服务。

2. 东台路的装饰艺术。

一直以来我最喜欢的上海购物经历是在东台路。古董摊上摆满的多是些俗气的古玩。但也有许多商店专卖上海艺术装饰品，价格合理，也稍有些讲价余地。两家分别叫上海艺术装饰和现代上海的商店特别棒。

3. 泽家居，丰华公路558号，靠近新福路。

买1910到1950年间顶尖品质的上海艺术装饰品，另一优良选择是泽家居。这一历史时期的上海工艺有很多独特精品，受传统中式图案如仙鹤、琼花造型的影响，它与其他地区的装饰艺术很不

同。价格比上海别的地方高，但与其首屈一指的质量相称。

4. 阁棂古董 嘉松中路4877号。

阁棂古董是一个十万平方英尺的大型展示厅，陈列着不同地区和时期的古董。这里可供选择的极多，你要预留充分时间去探索，因为那儿数不清的产品真是排山倒海地映入眼帘。

5. 上海木蓝花阁家具丽，济阳路1788号，近上浦路。

有些人喜欢到一个干净整洁、安排有致的美丽空间去买古董。如果你也是这样的人，请远离这个地方，它就如同自己的名字一般的冗长混乱。这片广阔空地货仓垒了20米高的成堆家具：大量的箱子、椅子、桌子、梯子、凳子和佛像，全部都给很大的讲价余地。从一堆垃圾里掘宝，找到你梦想的古董珍奇，运到家里之前，让这里友好的工作人员为你把它清洁干净。

Former French concession

法租界旧梦

To be honest this district is not my favorite place because I did not come to China to experience a similar atmosphere that I could find in my own country. The French Concession is like a small Paris.

The French Concession was established in 1849, when the French obtained a proclamation from the Governor (Daotai) of Shanghai, conceding certain territory for a French settlement.

The French Concession remained largely unchanged in the early decades of the Communist rule in China. In the late 1980s and the early 1990s, unregulated re-development of the area began tearing apart many neighbourhoods. The old French Club building and its gardens, which used to be a sports field in the early days, were gutted and became the base of the high-rise Okura Garden Hotel. After the 2000s, the government implemented more stringent development and planning regulations in the area.

Today, this Historic district is full of western style restaurants, small bistros, bars and

shops. The list of the historical restaurants is lengthy (Sasha's, Le Bouchon, etc.) althy Chinese and foreigners used to frequent this trendy area to enjoy a more Western ambience. Every corner is rich with stories of gangsters, amazing old houses, consular residences, and even some obscure tales of ghosts haunting their old houses where they were killed.

说实话，我并不太喜欢花时间在法租界逛，因为我来中国可不是为了体验一个与我自己国家相似的环境氛围。法租界给我的感觉就像个小巴黎。

法租界成立于 1849 年，法国人从上海道台手中获得公告，随后划定部分领土为法国人定居地。中国人民共和国成立初的几十年，法租界基本上保持不变。然而，1980 年代末和 1990 年代初，这区域缺乏管制的二次开发开始拆散众多居民区。比如，1990 年代砍除让曾经的霞飞路（现在淮海路）优雅生辉的伦敦梧桐，公众强烈抗议下才移回补种。老法国俱乐部和它的花园，早年间曾是运动场，被拆毁盖成了高耸的上海花园饭店。最后，2013 年，原先的英国大使馆成了洲际酒店。2000 年代以后，政府在这一区域实施了更严格的发展和规划管理。

今天，这一历史地区充满了西式餐厅、小酒馆、酒吧和商店。这里有一长串的历史餐厅 (Sasha’s，Le Bouchon 等。) 为享受西方情调，富裕的中国人和外国人过去常去这片时髦区。每个角落都满载故事，关于黑帮，不凡老宅，领事居所，甚至些朦胧含糊的鬼故事，被杀之人在老房子阴魂不散什么的。

Tea shop: "Song Fang Maison de Thé"

宋芳茶馆

Tea is considered one of the seven necessities of Chinese life, along with firewood, rice, oil, salt, soy sauce, and vinegar.

Tea was first brewed in 2737 B.C. and was discovered by the Emperor Shennong. To discover tea with a modern approach in Shanghai, I suggest you visit the Song Fang Maison de Thé, which specializes in the finest quality Chinese and French teas.

It was founded in Shanghai in 2007 by Florence Samson, a Paris native and a Shanghai resident for more than ten years. Her Chinese name is Song Fang (Song, from the Song dynasty and Fang meaning fragrant and of good repute).

This French lady, with a strong academic background, made her first contact with Asia in 1990 when she studied at Hitotsubashi University in Japan. It was then that she discovered the martial arts; she now has a black belt in Taekwondo. She worked for Dior cosmetics in Russia and China before becoming General Manager of Veuve Clicquot in China. She left the LVMH group to start the Song Fang Tea Company, as she wanted to share her passion for premium teas and the Chinese culture. Tea was invented in China and Chinese farmers have lovingly tended and harvested tea trees for nearly 5000 years. Song Fang is a tribute to those farmers.

The shop offers seventy kinds of tea from France and China and also some signature blends like the one I use to cook Etna, not strong but, of course, smoky. In 2009, my wife brought me a sample of my favorite mild and smoky black tea from this stop called Lapsong Sushong.

The reason this shop is so interesting lies not just in the tea but also in the story of the founder.

简言之，茶是中国人七种生活必需品之一，与柴、米、油、盐、酱和醋一样在中国人的生活中扮演着重要的角色。

茶是在公元前 2737 年，由神农制作的。在上海，如果你希望去品尝和探索茶的现代意义，我建议你去宋芳茶馆，那儿有最佳品质的中国和法国茶。

宋芳茶馆于 2007 年由法国人 Florence Samson 和一个上海人创立。Florence Samson 中文名叫宋芳（宋，指的是宋朝；芳，意味着香气和好名声）。这个法国女士，有着优秀的学历背景，她首次来到亚洲是在 1990 年，她在日本一桥大学 (Hitotsubashi University) 留学。就在那时，她深深地被武术吸引了，现在的她已经拿到了跆拳道黑带。Florence 起初在俄罗斯和中国为迪奥（法国时尚消费品牌）工作，后来又担任 LVMH 集团旗下凯歌香槟（世上第二大香槟制造商）的中国区总经理。为了要传播分享她对优质茶和对中国文化的热情，她离开了 LVMH 集团，创办了宋芳茶馆。

在中华文明的摇篮里诞生的茶在中国茶农的爱护照料下，茶文化已延绵 5000 年的历史。这家店提供来自法国和中国的七十种茶，也有一些独立品牌的混合茶，比如我在烹饪 Etna 时使用到的一种茶，它的味道不是很强烈，但是带着特有的烟熏味。2009 年，我的妻子在这家店给我带了些我最爱的口味淡淡、有烟熏味的黑茶，叫做 Lapsong Sushong。

这家店的魅力不单单在于它提供优质的茶，也在于其创始人的故事。

Recipe 16
食谱 16

shanghai smoked tea blended duck breast
上海茶熏鸭胸

4 Servings

4 人份

Ingredients
配料

1 --- Whole boneless Rougie duck breasts 整块无骨露杰鸭胸

10 g ---------------- Rams Smoked tea spice rub 茶熏香料胶

100 g -- uncooked rice 生米

20 g --------- Loose-leaf lychee black tea leaves 荔枝红茶叶

2 ------------------- Whole star anise or 1teaspoon anise seeds
整块八角（或一茶匙大茴香籽）

3 g --------------------- Whole black peppercorns 整黑胡椒粒

2 -- Cinnamon sticks 肉桂条

Zest of 1/4 orange, removed in large strips
四分之一个橙的大片皮碎

Smoked keemun salt
烟熏祁门盐

5 g -- Tea 茶

50 g -- Rice 米

320 g -- Coarse salt 粗盐

Wooden chips to smoke 烟熏用的木碎

Directions
作法

1. Trim of the excess fat on the Rougie duck breasts. Score the skin lightly several times diagonally with a sharp knife. Cut deep enough to cut through the skin and into the layer of the fat, but not into the duck meat underneath. This will aid in draining the excess fat off during cooking.

修剪掉露杰鸭胸上多余的油脂。用锋利的刀轻轻在对角线上切几次。深切并切穿鸭皮，并刚好到达肥肉层，但不要切进鸭肉底部。这有助于烹饪时排出多余的油脂。

2. Rub the breasts with the lychee tea spice rub. Cover and refrigerate overnight.

When the duck is ready to be cooked, light the gill and heat until the coals became ashes. While the grill heats, place the rice, tea, star anise, pepper corns, cinnamon sticks, and orange zest on a large piece of heavy-duty aluminum foil. Fold over to make a loose packet; keep the edges over to seal. Cut several small holes in the packet to allow the release of the aromatic smoke.

用荔枝茶香料胶摩擦鸭胸，盖好放入冰箱放置一晚。

当准备要煮的时候，点燃烤架，加热至煤燃尽。当烤架变热后，放入大米，茶叶，八角，胡椒粒，肉桂条和橙皮在大片铝箔上，折好，制成松散的小包，把边角折好密封。在小包上切几个小洞，使香气得以释放。

3. When the coals became ashes, flatten the mound and place the tea spice packet on the top of the coals with the holes facing upward.

当煤燃尽是，把其压平，放上茶叶香料包在煤上面，留洞朝下。

4. When the packet has begun to smoke, place the duck skin side down, on the grill, cook over medium heat, covered. Turn after around after 8 minutes and continue to cook, covered, until medium-rate, 55oC to 60oC using an instant-read thermometer.

当料包开始冒烟时，放上鸭胸，皮朝下，中火煮。盖好盖子。8分钟后翻转，然后继续煮，盖上盖子。煮至 55–60 摄氏度左右 – 查看温度计。

5. Remove the duck from the grill and let it rest for several minutes on a cutting board, tented with foil to keep warm. Slice the duck diagonally and serve immediately.

从烤架上移开鸭肉，放在砧板上几分钟，用铝箔罩着保温，对角线切片并马上上菜。

6. Smoked tea: Blend the rice to make it thin. Add the tea and the salt; put the blend in a stainless bowl and get a bigger bowl to contain the wooden chips. Light a fire to the chips and wrap all the stainless steel bowls to keep the smoke inside. Leave it like that for 15 minutes.

烟熏茶叶：把大米搅拌成细颗粒，加入茶叶和盐，把混合物放入不锈钢碗里，在另一个大一点的碗里放入木碎，点燃，包裹好整个不锈钢锅使烟保留在锅里面。静置 15 分钟。

Your notes

Great recipes are not created, but perfected.
好的食谱来自一次又一次的修改完善。

Note down the changes you make on this recipe to create your very own version of it.
记录下你对这个食谱做的修改，探寻属于你自己的味道。

Chef's tips
厨师贴士

I choose for this recipe the duck from the Rougie duck farm in China because the quality of the meat is exceptional on the Chinese mainland. The origin of the duck is from France and the feeding process is safe compared with most farms in China.

我选择上法国露杰品牌的鸭来制作该菜是因为其肉质在中国大陆来非常的好。他们鸭苗来自法国，喂养程序也相比其他养殖场更安全。

M50

M50 创意园

M50 (50 Moganshan Road) is one of Shanghai's most influential art centers with 130 artists and artist organizations from within China, and from over twenty countries and regions, on site.

The way M50 was formed is in fact is similar to New York's SOHO and Beijing's 798. Established in 2000, M50 has kept intact the unique factory buildings of China's national textile industry built between the 1930s and the 1990s. In the late 1990s, the textile enterprises started to move out of the city as a result of Shanghai's move to readjust its industrial structure. The abandoned factory buildings were put up for rent. Attracted by cheap rent, artists moved to Morganshan Road. That was the humble beginnings of M50, one of the earliest clusters in Shanghai. Today, the clustering effect has enabled M50 to expand from an artist precinct to a creative cluster that involves a variety of sectors. It has established a complete industrial chain as well as an operating model in which similar industries concentrate, and in which different industries complement each other.

M50 创意园（莫干山路 50 号），上海最具影响力的艺术中心之一，这里有 130 名艺术家和艺术家组织，来自中国及超过 20 个国家和地区。M50 形成的方式实际上类似于纽约苏荷区和北京的 798。成立于 2000 年，M50 将独特的中国国家纺织工业建筑保存完好，这些建筑建于 1930 年代到 1990 年代间。1990 年代末，由于产业结构调整，纺织企业开始搬出城区。这个废弃的厂房出租。艺术家们为便宜的租金所吸引，纷纷搬到莫干山路。作为上海最早的集群之一，这便是 M50 卑微的起始。今天，集群效应使得 M50 从单纯艺术家聚集区扩展成了一个涉及众多行业的创意产业园区。它建立了一个完整的产业链和一个良好的运营模式，让同类产业集聚，不同产业互补。

Rooftop gardens

空中花园

In Shanghai I used to climb tall buildings and I was very surprised to discover very often some gardens or trees on the roof top of brand new buildings. There are already 500,000 square meters of rooftop gardens in Minhang District alone.

Many of the district's government buildings, schools and hospitals have grass, shrubs or small trees on their rooftops, which make the buildings cooler during the hot summer. This I believe is also part of Shanghai's aspiration to go green and ecological. In some areas in Shanghai, the building owners would plant some fruit trees and vegetables. Each apartment owner can get their own space to collect their vegetables or fruits. If all the buildings are covered with roof top gardens, the city temperature could drop several degrees.

在上海我经常会攀爬高大的建筑。非常令我惊奇的是，在一些全新的大楼顶部通常都会有一个屋顶花园或栽种着一些树木。现在单在闵行地区，屋顶花园的面积就有 50 万平米。闵行地区的政府大楼，各个学校和医院在楼顶一般都会种植草皮，灌木或者是较为低矮的树木，这样在炎热的夏季整栋楼会感觉较为凉爽。我想这也应该是上海绿色生态蓝图中的部分规划。在上海一些地区，一些楼主也会在楼顶种植果树，或者蔬菜，这样户主就可以自给自足满足平时的生活需求了。如果是上海市所有的房顶都带这样的空中花园，整个城市的温度肯定能下降好几度。

The Night Life

不夜城

The list of places you can go at a Shanghai night goes on and on:
夜行上海好去处

Stylish 24-hour restaurants 二十四小时营业的高雅餐厅

Street food plazas 小吃广场 Bars and jazz clubs 酒吧，爵士俱乐部

Night clubs with popular international DJ 知名国际 DJ 入驻的夜店

SPAs 疗养中心 Opera, cinema, theater houses 剧院，电影院，戏院

KTVs 歌厅 Concerts and festivals 音乐会，节日庆典

Dance shows 舞蹈表演 River cruises 水上夜游

International entertainment shows 国际娱乐表演

Roller skating, snooker, bowling 溜冰，台球，保龄球

Shanghai probably has the most colorful nightlife in China. But if you have really tried one, you might think it probably has the most colorful one in the world.

But like in all the big cities, the business opens and closes. One day a place is trendy and hot; the next day it is gone. That's why the business owners always try to be more creative and think of new ideas to attract more customers. The best places are the ones you can find the right cultural mix, with foreigners and Chinese who really appreciate and enjoy the ambiance of this city.

上海大概是中国夜生活最丰富多彩的地方。你要是有去过亲自体验过的话，你也许会觉，就算说它是世界夜生活最多样化的地方一点都不夸张。

但是正如其它的大城市一样，这里的店铺更新变化的速度非常的快。前天你还见到那里有一家非常时髦的门面，第二天它就消失得无影无踪了。这也就是为什么上海的商家们一直绞尽脑汁，想着如何来用创意来吸引更多的顾客。一家出色的店铺应该善于平衡，融合不同的文化氛围，在这里不管是外国客人还是本土的顾客都能惬意地体会，享受到上海大都市的氛围。

In the early 20th century, Shanghai has been called the Paris of the east, now they are saying it is China's New York. Shanghai is one of the world's greatest cities with an amazing night life. It's the sleepless city in China.

二十世纪早期的时候，上海被称作为"东方巴黎"。而在现代，它则叫做"东方纽约"。作为世界最大城市之一，它有着非常棒的夜生活，堪称是中国的不夜城。

Shanghai is also a city filled with surprises

上海是惊喜不断的城市

There are many underground bars where local and foreigners share a pint of beer, chat, gossip and dance.

The most surprising place was for me the Mansion near Hongqiao Lu and Hongjing Lu. It is in the middle of extravagant villas, where the luxuries cars owners having a good time with all those young trendy artists in huge houses. Several years ago the owner of Mansion decided to create a place where artists, DJ, Skaters can communicate and share their talents. There is a basement where the DJ can go crazy, a backyard with a pool and a beach area, a bar space, and even rooms where you can stay the whole night.

Downtown you can find some concert halls like the Yuyintang which is one of the oldest underground live music houses in Shanghai, and has become a must-visit spot in the city. Featuring regular gigs every weekend, it brings in underground rock acts both worldwide and local. The Spartan décor is similar to concert houses you can find only in New York or London. This place is an example of a perfect melting pot in Shanghai.

One of my most memorable moments in Shanghai was climbing the top buildings at night. The city looked astonishing from the roofs of the skyscrapers. I spent some time at night climbing the top building in China, which was like a sort of urban trekking where the risks were rewarded by the breathtaking views.

这里有很多的地下酒吧，本地和外国人在这里喝啤酒，聊天，八卦和跳舞。对我来说，最特别的地方是大厦附近的虹桥路和虹景路。它们位于高档别墅中间，名牌汽车车主们和这些年轻有才华的艺术家一起有充足的时间在宽敞的空间里交流。几年前，大厦的业主决定腾出一个地方专给艺术家，DJ，选手们交流和分享他们才华的地方。这还有一个 DJ 们可以去疯一下地方 -- 地下室，后院有游泳池和海滩区，酒吧，甚至还有你可以呆上一整晚的房间。

市中心可以找到一些音乐厅，比如育音堂，它是上海历史最悠久的地下现场音乐之一，也是来上海不可错过的一个地方。育音堂每到周末都会有常规的演出，它融合了全球和地方的地下摇滚元素。在这里你可以找到只有在纽约或伦敦才可以欣赏到的斯巴达装饰的演唱会房子。这完美地呈现了上海文化艺术大熔炉的形象。

我在上海最难忘的一段时光是晚上去爬摩天大楼。从楼顶往下看，这座城市实在太迷人了。不知有多少个晚上我是在爬高楼大厦中度过的，很刺激，感觉就像在城市里体验野外的徒步冒险，眼前的美景便是我能得到的最好的犒劳。

The Mokkos Bar

Mokkos 酒吧

The Japanese style bar Mokkos stands out for its perfect ethnic mix and its small cozy environment, with great drinks, service and ambiance. It is located in an alleyway. When you walk inside you will discover a small bar with only a few wooden tables. This place is always packed with the bar's regular customers, most of whom speak Chinese and have their own bottles or glass in the place with their special beverages requests. Some of them play guitar, singing with the bar's manager Lamu who is from Nepal and hired by the former Japanese bar owners. Back then she did not speak much Chinese but the guests adored her right away, not only for her sweet smiles but also because of her talent in singing. This place is a must-visit place in Shanghai if you want to skip the crowded clubs and bars to simply enjoy a great time in a Shanghai bar

隐藏于小巷子里的 Mokkos 日式酒吧有着不一样的热闹，这里聚集着形形色色的人来自不同的国家和文化，还有美酒饮料任君选择，服务周到之余还有让人乐而忘返的舒适氛围。小小的地方只有几张木桌，却总是坐满了这里的常客，不需要过多询问，服务员就知道他们喜好的饮品。这里大部分人都会讲中文。有些客人在弹吉他，和酒吧经理 Luma 一起高歌。这位经理是尼泊尔人，受雇于之前酒吧的日本老板。虽然她不太会讲中文，但是却深得客人喜爱，她总是笑容满面，歌又唱得特别好。如果你不想去那些拥挤的夜总会或者酒吧，那就不要错过这个上海酒吧纯粹的欢乐时光。

Must-try Shanghainese Dishes

一定要试的上海小吃

城隍庙店
加盟
台湾士林小吃
门面转租
13917559193

When you come to Shanghai, do not miss the chance to go to famous Shanghai Cuisine restaurants and try the signature local dishes.

You should try the famous Nanxiang steamed stuffed buns, crab-yellow pastry, fried stuffed buns, chop rice cake, vegetable stuffed buns, Leisha dumplings and wontons. Various snack streets in the city have many restaurants and eateries to tempt you. Wujiang Road, Old Town God Temple Snack Street, South Yunnan Road and Xianxia Road are the best among them.

当你来到上海，千万不要错过机会去著名的上海菜餐厅，并尝试签名当地菜肴。

你应该尝试著名的南翔小笼包子，蟹黄色的糕点，油炸包子，砍年糕，蔬菜馅的包子，饺子蕾莎和馄饨。各种小吃街 在城市有许多餐馆和饮食店诱惑你。吴江路，老城隍庙小吃街，南云南路和仙霞路是其中最好的。

“When I worked in Shanghai a guest asked me where he could find a good restaurant. My answer was :“Just go across the street and enjoy the real Chinese street food.”

在上海工作的时候，有一位客人问我在哪里可以找到一个很好的餐馆。我的回答是：“...... 就在马路对面，那里就有地道的中国街边小吃 ......”

Directory
相关地址信息

1. Linlong Fang Xiaolongbao

10 Jianguo Dong Lu, Near Zhaozhou Lu

Tel 21 6386 7021

1. 麟笼坊小笼包

上海建国东路 10 号，临近肇周路

电话：2163867021

2. Crab Fairyland

Right by the Yangcheng Lake. Good crabs, even better chicken and pumpkin congee.

3338 Hubin Nan Lu, Bacheng.

2.Crab Fairyland

位于阳澄湖边。蟹质很好，那里的鸡肉、南瓜更胜一筹。

苏州市巴城镇湖滨南路 3338 号

3. Lotus

Hubei soul food: pure soups, steamed meats, hearty ganguo (dry pot stews).

641 Changning Lu, near Anxi Lu.

3. 莲花餐厅

湖北菜精华：纯汤，蒸肉，丰盛干锅。

长宁路 641 号。临近安西路

4. Yu Xin Chuan Cai

An upscale chain from Chongqing, keeping the original Sichuan flavor.

3/F, 333 Chengdu Bei Lu, near Weihai Lu.

Tel 5298 0438.

4. 渝信川菜

来自重庆，秉承四川菜传统的高档连锁餐馆，味道正宗。

成都北路 333 号 3 层，临近威海路

电话：52980438

5. Yershari

High quality Xinjiang chain restaurant

Whole lambs, tiny grapes, flatbreads, kitsch decor and strong cumin taste.

411 Tianlin Dong Lu, near Qinzhou Lu.

Tel 6451 9797

5. 耶里夏丽新疆餐厅

新疆菜新锐连锁餐厅，特色烤全羊，小葡萄，小面包干；装潢简，孜然味浓。

田林东路 411 号，临近钦州路

电话：64519797

6. Lan Gui Fang

Premium SH'nese noodle shop with communal tables, no-nonsense service and excellent clam noodles.

417Loushanguan Lu, near Xianxia Lu.

Tel 6274 0084.

6. 兰桂坊酒家

优质的上海特色面店，店内桌子公用，服务良好，蛤蜊面相当优秀。

娄山关路 417 号，临近仙霞路

电话：62740084

7. Tonkatsu Hamachan

Great Japanese place, fried pork cutlet shop with a convenient location.

176 Jiaozhou Lu, near Beijing Xi Lu. Tel 6256 8674

7. 浜崎猪排

很不错的日本菜馆，主营炸猪排，交通方便。

胶州路 176 号，临近北京西路

电话：62568674

8. Nanling

Garish Yangzhou workhorse with amazing "lion's head" meatballs and decent roast duck.

168 Yueyang Lu, near Yongjia Lu.

Tel 6467 7381

8. 南伶酒家

装修花哨的扬州菜馆，红烧狮子头做得无与伦比，还有不错的烤鸭

岳阳路 168 号，临近永嘉路

电话：64677381

9. Golden Anchor

Old Shanghainese style restaurant that has good soy-seasoned sticky rice with roe crabs.

543 Xinhua Lu, near Dingxi Lu.

Tel 5258 1097

9. 金锚传菜

旧上海的风格、蟹子酱糯米饭味道很好，新华路 543 号，临近定西路。

电话：52581097

10. Charmant

Taiwanese comfort food that opens until 4 a.m. Good three-cup chicken, soaring shaved ice desserts.

1414 Huaihai Zhong Lu, near Fuxing Xi Lu.

Tel 6431 8107

10. 小城故事 徐汇店

舒适的台湾菜馆，营业到凌晨四点。三杯鸡和刨冰甜点不错

淮海中路 1414 号，临近复兴西路

电话：64318107

11. Lan Ting

Grimy hole-in-the-wall with a constant line for sweet, sweet homestyle Shanghainese cooking. Jigu jiang is the star. 107 Songshan Lu, near Taicang Lu. Tel 5306 9650

11. 兰亭餐厅

店面面积狭小，甚至有点脏乱，但一直走的是温馨路线，提供温馨上海住家菜吗，还有特色鸡骨酱

嵩山路 107 号，临近太仓路

电话：53069650

12. Chun

Four tables family-style restaurant that doesn't even have no menu.

124 Jinxian Lu, near Maoming Nan Lu.

Tel 6256 0301

12. 春餐厅

私房菜餐馆，里面只有四张餐桌，没有菜单。家庭式风格。

进贤路 124 号，临近茂名南路

电话：62560301

13. Mao Long

Storefront restaurant, home-style Shanghainese. Neighbor to Chun.

134 Jinxian Lu, near Maoming Nan Lu.

Tel 6256 1167

13. 茂隆餐厅

私房菜餐馆，上海家庭式的布局，进贤路 134 号，临近春餐厅

电话：62561167

14. Lan Xin

Storefront restaurant, home-style Shanghainese.

Neighbor to Chun and Mao Long. 130 Jinxian Lu, near Maoming Nan Lu, Tel 6253 3554

14. 兰心餐厅

私房菜餐馆，上海家庭式布局，进贤路 134 号，临近春餐厅和茂隆餐厅。

电话：62533554

15. Xin Guang Jiu Jia

Seasonal hairy crab popular restaurant. Open only in autumn.

512 Tianjin Lu, near Guangxi Bei Lu. Tel 6322 3978

15. 新光酒家

星级大闸蟹，只在秋天营业。

天津路 512 号，临近广西北路

电话：63223978

16. Tentekomai

Solid izakaya with standout miniature gyoza.

242 Julu Lu, near Ruijin Yi Lu. Tel 5228 0650

16. 天手古舞

一家厚实的居酒屋，供应特色的日式小饺子。巨鹿路 242 号，临近瑞金一路。

电话：52280650

17. Toriyasu

The best of Shanghai's many yakitori stores. The setting is smoky, dim, lively.

890 Changning Lu, near Huichuan Lu (entrance on Huichuan). Tel 5241 1677

17. 鸟安

最好的上海日式烤串，店内烟雾弥漫，灯管昏暗，但生气十足。长宁路 890 号，临近汇川路（汇川路入口）

电话：52411677

18. San Gu Bullfrog

No-frills bullfrog restaurant. The best is the Sichuan-style frog with lotus root, potato chips, fermented black beans, lettuce stem, ginger, and chili. 883 Zhaojiabang Lu, near Wanping Lu. Tel 6469 4611.

18. 三顾牛蛙

专营牛蛙的餐厅，店内朴实，没有刻意的装潢。最好吃的是川味牛蛙，配料包括莲藕，土豆片，酿黑豆，莴苣茎，姜，辣椒。

肇嘉浜路 883 号，临近宛平路

电话：64694611

19. Fu 1088

Precise, contemporary Shanghainese restaurant in a 20's villa. 375 Zhenning Lu, near Yuyuan Lu. Tel 5239 7878.

19. 福 1088

正宗的当代上海餐馆，位于一座 20 世纪 20 年代的别墅内，镇宁路 375 号，临近愚园路。

电话：52397878

20. Palace Duck

Pressure-fried duck, cooked in a supposedly imperial palace style. Takeaway stall only. 311 Xiangyang Nan Lu, near Yongjia Lu.

20. 皇宫爆烤鸭

采用传说中宫廷秘方卤汁腌制，爆烤而成。仅外卖，无堂食。

襄阳南路 311 号，临近永嘉路

21. Friday Muslim Market

Changde Lu in between Aomen Lu and Yichang Lu

21. 星期五穆斯林集市

常德路，澳门路与宜昌路之间

22. Qibao Old Street Tangyuan

"Old China" water town street, genuinely delicious sticky rice dumplings with jujube, black sesame fillings.

22. 七宝旧街汤圆

这里是“旧中国”的水乡一条街，里面有卖正宗美味的糯米汤圆，馅料主要有枣，黑芝麻。

23. Sushi Haru

2088 Intimate, upscale sushi that opens until 4a.m.

The back side of 2088 Yan'an Xi Lu, near Yili Nan Lu.

Tel 6173 8288.

23. 鮨春

高档寿司餐厅，营业至凌晨 4 点。位于延安西路 2088 号后座，临近伊犁南路

电话：61738288

24. Tianshan Tea City

Four floor tea market.

24. 天山茶城

四层楼的茶叶市场

25. Da Ke Tang Pu'er Teahouse

Elite teahouse in a handsome restored villa, focusing on expensive pu'er -- the Bordeaux of tea.

Lane 388 Xiangyang Nan Lu,

near Yongfu Lu. Tel 6467 6577.

25. 大可堂普洱茶馆

这是上海的精品茶馆，位于一座漂亮的度假别墅中，专注于昂贵的普洱茶—茶中的波尔多酒。

襄阳南路 388 弄 25 号，临近永福路。

26. Fengjing Town

Most of the restaurant on the river side offer local specialties, simple but fresh.

26. 枫泾古镇

河岸边的大多数餐馆都有当地特色菜，菜式简单但是新鲜。

27. Mokkos Bar

Not easy to find but unique, only regular customers know about this place.

Liquors, cocktails and Japanese drinks

Rm 201, 1245 Wuding Xi lu near Wanhangdu lu

Tel 6212 1114

27.Mokkos 酒吧

找到这里不容易，这里气氛相当特别，只有常客知道这个地方。

烈酒、鸡尾酒和日本酒

武定西路 1245 号 201 房，临近万航渡路

电话：62121114

28. Propaganda posters and art museum

It's in a building in the cave area that looks like a underground place.

Unique exhibition of original posters about the Communism propaganda.

The owner sell some original pieces all around the world.

868 Huashan Rd, Xuhui, Shanghai, China

Tel 6211 1845

Sunday hours 10:00 am–5:00 pm

28. 上海宣传画艺术中心

这座建筑修建在一个洞穴区域内，看起来像是在地下世界。这里是独一无二的共产党宣传画展览室。

主人也会向世界各地售卖一些原创的作品

徐汇区华山路 868 号

电话：6211 1845

周日营业时间：10:00am–5:00pm

29. YuyinTang Live House

It's one of the oldest Concert house in Shanghai, music stage, graffiti on the walls, nice atmosphere, good mix with local and foreigners. Chinese rock groups shows.

851 Kaixuan Lu, by Yan'an Xi Lu Tel 5237 8662

29. 上海育音堂

这是上海最老的音乐厅之一，里面有音乐舞台，墙上有涂鸦，气氛很好，当地人与外国人在这里相处融合得很好。这里也有中国的摇滚乐队演出。

凯旋路 851 号，临近延安西路

电话：52378662

Acknowledgement

致谢

My family

My parents have been the very first inspiration for me to write this book. The different cultural origins I learned about from them make it possible for me to embrace the diverse cultures of different peoples, which has helped me enormously in my career and my life.

My Wife Donia who is my "mental coach", my precious inspiration, who is always there for me, supporting me in each and every one of my adventure. With Donia, I will share my passion for food in the next book about Guangzhou.

My friends

I want to thank Pascal Boucon from "Food In" who has been my friends for years, for showing me the lesser-travelled places in Shanghai and sharing with me his thorough understanding of this Chinese city.

My thanks also goes to Chef Johnson Sun, who was a great company to my many journeys in Shanghai, the two Michelin stars chef Nicolas Le Bec, the talented culinary photographer Vincent Ho, and Didier Corlou, Chef in Hanoi Vietnam who has enlightened me on the great knowledge involving the balanced diet in Asian cuisines. And of course Franck Lafourcade with whom I shared my first Asian experience in Shanghai when I worked for him.

My editor

Last but not least, I am grateful to the editorial and production team at SendPoints Publishing for their professional expertise.

I am also indebted to many who have kindly helped me in my trips exploring Shanghai.

我的家人

这本书最初的创作灵感来自于我的父母。我从他们那里了解到不同文化的起源，这使得我可以去包容各民族多样性的文化，并给我的职业生涯和生活都带来了很大的帮助。

我的妻子 Donia 永远在背后支持着我，对我的每一次冒险也都持肯定意见，她是我最真诚的精神导师和最珍贵的灵感来源。在我下一本关于广州的书里，我会继续跟我的妻子一起与大家分享我对烹饪的热情。

我的朋友们

我想对我的老朋友，Food In 公司的 Pascal Boucon 真心地说声谢谢，是他向我介绍了上海那些我鲜少涉足的地方，还与我分享了他对上海这座中国城市的理解。

此外，我还要感谢 Johnson Sun 大厨。我在上海的多次出行都是在他的陪同之下进行的。

另外，我还要感谢米其林二星大厨 Nicolas Le Bec 和才华横溢的烹饪摄影师 Vincent Ho 一路上给我的支持。越南河内的大厨 Didier Corlou 在亚洲菜的均衡饮食这一方面，给了我很多启发。当然还有 Franck Lafourcade。在我为他工作的期间，是他和我走过了亚洲之旅的始发站—上海站。

我的编辑

我非常感激善本出版公司的编辑和出版团队在本书出版工作上提供的专业帮助。

最后，我想把我最诚挚的谢意献给那些在我探访上海期间帮助过我的每一个人。

With this book I hope some of you will have another vision of the megalopolis and see a different portray of the Shanghainese people.

Shanghai is still in my heart the City where my daughter was born, the first city where I started my work in Asia and of course the first land that opened up my eyes to appreciate a different culture.

希望这本书能给你一个不同的视角去看待上海这个大都市，去了解不一样的上海生活。在我心里，上海始终有着一个特别的位置：这里是我女儿出生的地方，是我在亚洲工作的第一个城市。这个美丽的城市也鼓励了我，让我继续去探寻不同的文化、不一样的味道。

上海本真

—法国大厨的中国美食之旅

SHANGHAI FLAIR

— The Vision of a French Chef in China

Author: Nicolas A. VIENNE
作者：Nicolas A. VIENNE　EMAIL/ 邮箱：nicvienne@hotmail.com

PUBLISHED BY SendPoints Publishing Co., Ltd.
善本出版有限公司出版

PUBLISHER: Lin Gengli
出版人：林庚利

PUBLISHING DIRECTOR: Lin Shijian
出版总监：林诗健

EDITOR: Sundae Li
编辑：李庄庄

ART EDITOR: Peng Lingbo
美术编辑：彭凌波

ART DIRECTOR: He Wanling
美术指导：何婉玲

ADDRESS: Room 15A Block 9 Tsui Chuk Garden, Wong Tai Sin, Kowloon, Hong Kong
地址：香港九龙黄大仙翠竹花园 9 座 15A

TEL/ 电话：+852-35832323　FAX/ 传真：+852-35832448

EMAIL/ 邮箱：info@sendpoints.cn

DISTRIBUTED BY Guangzhou SendPoints Book Co., Ltd.
广州善本图书有限公司发行

SALES MANAGER: Zhang Juan (China), Sissi (International)
销售经理：张娟（中国）李晓茜（海外）

GUANGZHOU 广州电话：+86-20-89095121
BEIJING 北京电话：+86-10-84139071
SHANGHAI 上海电话：+86-21-63523469
EMAIL/ 邮箱：overseas01@sendpoints.cn
WEBSITE/ 网站：www.sendpoints.cn
ONLINE STORE/ 官方网店：shanbents.tmall.com

ISBN 978-988-13834-0-2